Black Feminist Voices
in Politics

Black Feminist Voices in Politics

Evelyn M. Simien

State University of New York Press

Image courtesy of The Amistad Center for Art & Culture at the Wadsworth Atheneum Museum of Art, Hartford, CT. Carrie Mae Weems, American, b. 1953 May Flowers from May Days Long Forgotten, 2003 C-print, wood and convex glass Collection of The Amistad Center for Art & Culture, AF 2004.1.1

Published by
State University of New York Press, Albany

© 2006 State University of New York

For information, address State University of New York Press,
194 Washington Avenue, Suite 305, Albany, NY 12210-2384

Production by Kelli Williams
Marketing by Susan Petrie

Library of Congress Cataloging-in-Publication Data

Simien, Evelyn M., 1974–
    Black feminist voices in politics / Evelyn M. Simien.
        p. cm.
    Includes bibliographical references and index.
    ISBN 0-7914-6789-9 (hardcover : alk. paper) — ISBN 0-7914-6790-2 (pbk. : alk. paper)   1. Feminism—United States—History   2. African American women—United States—Social conditions.   3. Women in politics—United States.   I. Title.

HQ1410.S56 2006
323.196'073'0082—

                                                                    2005023938
                        10 9 8 7 6 5 4 3 2 1

To my parents, Mearline LeDee Simien and Lawrence Simien

For my nephews, Douglas, Dustin, Gabe, and Isaiah

CONTENTS

Acknowledgments

1   Charting a Course for Black Women's Studies in   1
Political Science

2   From Margin to Center: African American Women   19
and Black Feminist Theory

3   Race Trumps Gender or Vice Versa? Cross Pressures   41
and Deliberate Choices

4   Black Feminist Consciousness and Its Determinants: 63
Factors Rooted in Experience

5   Black Feminist Consciousness, Race Consciousness,   93
and Black Political Behavior

6   The Future of Feminist Scholarship and Black   119
Politics Research

Epilogue: Stablility and Change in Attitudes toward   139
Black Feminism

Appendix A: Black Feminist Consciouness   157

Appendix B: Determinants of Black Feminist   159
Consciousness

Appendix C: Race Consciousness   163

Appendix D: Political Behavior   165

References   167

Index   185

ACKNOWLEDGMENTS

I am indebted to many people who have supported me throughout the process of writing this book. I am very grateful for the financial support provided to me initially by my dissertation advisor, William R. Shaffer, in the Department of Political Science at Purdue University, who sponsored me for the Purdue Research Foundation Grant. The grant is an assistantship awarded on a competitive basis to support dissertation thesis research. I am forever indebted to William Shaffer for assisting me in the development and execution of this project as he read the manuscript in its earliest stages. I am equally indebted to Rosalee A. Clawson who never wavered in her faith in this project, even as she insisted that I revise and edit drafts. I have truly benefited from her insightful critiques, practical guidance, and careful instruction. To date, she has served as a role model and life coach. Rosie recognized me as a legitimate scholar, encouraged me to engage in professional activities, and taught me how to succeed in graduate school. I must thank Michael A. Weistein and S. Laurel Weldon for their helpful comments and thoughtful suggestions as they too served on my dissertation committee. Other faculty, namely, Floyd Hayes and Diane Rubenstein, provided me with tremendous support throughout the course of my graduate career. The hours they spent talking with me about their ideas, experiences, and frustrations inspired me in countless ways.

I am especially appreciative of the frank advice and challenging questions I received from Richard Brown, Charles Menifield, Nancy Naples, Howard Reiter, and Katherine Tate. I owe a special note of gratitude to Richard Brown, Director of the University of Connecticut's Humanities Institute, who generously agreed to take time from his busy schedule to discuss the ideas presented here. He proved to be a sharp and careful reader of the large faculty research grant, which received support from the University of Connecticut's Research Foundation to fund the 2004–2005 National Black Feminist Study. Others either read individual chapters or the entire manuscript at various stages. Their comments helped strengthen the work in important ways.

I wish to thank my dear friends Nikol Alexander-Floyd, Natalie Barrett, Derrick Bellard, Sherman Benoit, Nicole Broussard, Randolph Burnside, Lawrence Davis, Elena Edwards, Duchess Harris, Rhasaan Hicks-Wilson, Linda Hood, Julia Jordan-Zachery, Sharon LaTour, Monica Patin, Linda Trautman, David Williams, and Michelle Williams, for their attentive ears and genuine counsel. I also wish to thank several members of my family—Joyce Ardoin, Candace Guillory, Patricia Guillory, Hayward and Marjorie Labbe, Demetria LeDay, Majesta and Clarence LeDee, and Pam Roy—for their unwavering support and unconditional love. I especially want to thank my fiancé, Steven King Jr., for the joy and balance he brings to my life. Finally, I must acknowledge my parents: Mearline LeDee Simien and Lawrence Simien have always demonstrated an honest commitment to my personal growth and development. In my judgment, they continue to uphold the highest moral and ethical standards. I aspire to do the same.

Chapter 1

CHARTING A COURSE
FOR BLACK WOMEN'S STUDIES
IN POLITICAL SCIENCE

Only the black woman can say, when and where I enter . . .
then and there the whole race enters with me.

> —Anna Julia Cooper, *A Voice from the South*

This book represents a conscious and deliberate effort to chart a course for black women's studies in political science. According to Mack Jones, distinguished professor of political science at Clark Atlanta University and founding president of the National Conference of Black Political Scientists, the responsibility of black political scientists is to "develop a political science which grows out of a black perspective" and so the chapters that follow are united by this goal (1977, 16). Understanding that it is important, but not enough, to say that the general concern from which the book originates is the paucity of scholarly research devoted to black feminist voices in politics, I maintain that the integration of leading historic black female activists aids in the explanation and understanding of group consciousness in general and black feminist consciousness in particular, as both are rooted in lived experiences with interlocking systems of oppression. Perhaps the best way to understand the simultaneity of oppression faced by black women is to study the proponents of black feminism as they engaged in public debate and grassroots activism, assuming that black feminist consciousness has in some ways shaped, or at least informed, their political activities in light of the historical contexts, material conditions, and lived experiences that beget their acute sense of awareness. For that reason, this chapter devotes scholarly attention to one of the first black female intellectuals to focus on the race-sex correspondence in black women's lives: Anna Julia Cooper.

As the quote at the beginning of this chapter suggests, the intellectual roots of black feminism and its relevance to politics go back a long way. Overcoming racism and sexism has had a profound impact on African American women, inspiring them to actively participate in tremendously successful grassroots campaigns. Starting with the antislavery and women's suffrage movements, black female activists were among the first to speak out against racial and sexual oppression in the United States (Lerner 1972; Shanley 1988; Terborg-Penn 1998; Olson 2001). Anna Julia Cooper's seminal work, *A Voice from the South*, is considered the earliest and most visible manifestation of black feminist consciousness. Writing in 1892, prior to W. E. B. DuBois's declaration that the problem of the twentieth century was the color line, Cooper asserted that women of African descent were "confronted by a woman question and a race problem" and remarked that "while our men seem thoroughly abreast of the times on every other subject, when they strike the woman question, they drop back into sixteenth century logic" (see Loewenberg and Bogin 1976, 244; Washington 1988, xxix; Cooper 1995, 45). Given her status as a member of the black intelligentsia, her comments call attention to the male-dominated character of black leadership and raise questions about conventional notions of respectable manhood and true womanhood at the turn of the century. Taken together, these statements capture the essence of black feminist thought as interlocking systems of oppression circumscribe the lives of African American women.

A consummate teacher, intellectual mind, and much sought after lecturer, Anna Julia Cooper was critical of educational systems that failed to consider the needs of African American women. Given that she subscribed to bourgeois notions of respectability and genteel femininity that prevented her from recognizing the intellectual and leadership abilities of black women laborers, Cooper advocated liberal arts education for black female elites (Giddings 1984; Guy-Sheftall 1995; Gaines 1996; James 1997; Olson 2001). Cooper opined, "We can't all be professional people. We must have a backbone to the race" (Giddings 1984, 103) and attributed agency to black women college graduates. Her condemnation of the women's movement and its leaders, Susan B. Anthony and Eliza- beth Cady Stanton, for their unwillingness to oppose racism in women's clubs was accepted and applauded by black male author- ity until she expressed disapproval of those conservative black male leaders who marginalized the plight and potential of black women in their discussions of the race problem (Harley and Terborg-Penn 1978; Giddings 1984; Guy-Sheftall 1995; Gaines 1996; James 1997). Despite an academic career that lasted longer than that of DuBois, her political philosophy on a variety of issues ranging from women's rights to black liberation and from segregation to literary criticism has been virtually ignored and forgotten by contemporary scholars. Cooper, whose political philosophy was ahead of her time, has not garnered nearly as much scholarly attention as her black male counterparts, although her scholarship and political ac- tivism compel juxtaposition with fellow black leaders, specifically DuBois in whom she found an ally (Harley and Terborg-Penn 1978; Giddings 1984; Gaines 1996; James 1997; Olson 2001).

While DuBois has long been viewed as an intellectual giant, Cooper has been largely ignored—unexamined. The mother of black feminism, Cooper deserves special recognition for her intellec- tual prowess. She was a well-respected figure during an intense pe- riod of civil rights activism, marking the rise of black female–led institutions and organizations (Harley and Terborg-Penn 1978; Gaines 1996; Olson 2001). Mirroring the reality of this black woman intellectual, as she has been effectively written out of history, black feminist theory has not garnered much scholarly attention in political science. That is to say, in spite of the progress that has been made in recent years, too few political scientists deem African Amer- ican women and black feminist theory worthy of intellectual inquiry. I am optimistic, however, that the present study will stimulate more theoretical and empirically based work on the subject.

Despite the emergence of the study of women and politics within the discipline of political science, efforts to transform the cur- riculum and integrate perspectives of African American women have met with limited success. Few political scientists have written books and journal articles about African American women as political actors—candidates for elective office, grassroots organizers, party activists, voters, or partisan, ideologically engaged citizens—when African American women have a long history of actively participating in politics via antislavery networks, civil rights organizations, and black feminist collectives (Collins 2000). Still, they remain largely invisible. The near absence of scholarship on and by African American women in political science constitutes a void in the literature. This book fills the void by drawing a material link between those who have written about African American women as political actors and those who have engaged in black feminist theorizing. It does not profess to be a comprehensive survey of black feminist scholarship; rather, it demonstrates ways in which black feminist theory can inform quantitative analyses of black attitudes toward gender equality and feminist priorities. Until recently, no black political scientists had examined the level of support for gender equality and feminist priorities among African American men and women. Only Michael C. Dawson (2001) and I (Simien 2001) have pursued this question by using a national survey of the adult African American population.

In his book *Black Visions,* Michael C. Dawson provides empirical evidence derived from the 1993–1994 National Black Politics Study (NBPS) to support his claim that contemporary black political preferences are related to various historical political ideologies (e.g., black Marxism, black nationalism, black feminism, black conservatism, disillusioned liberalism, and radical egalitarianism). In his chapter, "A Vision of Their Own: Identity and Black Feminist Ideology," Dawson (like myself) develops and validates a measure of black feminist consciousness that is true to its theoretical origins. He finds that black feminism has an important effect on blacks' perceptions of the desirability of multiracial coalitions (e.g., African Americans who support a black feminist ideology are most likely to support political alliances with individuals outside of the black community). For this reason, Dawson suggests that black feminism has the greatest potential to overcome social difference and bridge common humanity with the racial specificity of blackness as it recognizes interlocking systems of oppression (Fogg-Davis 2003). While Dawson's chapter has much to offer scholars doing empirical work on the simultaneity of oppression faced by black women, it falls short of providing a thorough and complete literature review that draws a material link between black feminist theorizing and mainstream political science.

Drawing on the same black feminist literature as I, Dawson determines that black feminist consciousness has three core ingredients: an understanding of intersectionality, a focus on community-centered politics, and an emphasis on the particular experiences of black women. However, he offers no review of the extant literature in political science relative to black feminism and his conceptualization of this construct as it differs from the mainstream conceptualization of group consciousness by political scientists. A unique and contrasting feature of my book, as compared to Dawson's chapter, is that I offer a particularly useful review of the literature on black feminist consciousness, gender (or feminist) consciousness, and race consciousness accompanied by an incisive critique of the dominant approaches used by political scientists to measure these specific strands of group consciousness. I consider all three bodies of literature in my effort to present both a broad and a balanced assessment of black feminist consciousness. The advantage to this approach is that black feminist consciousness is discussed relative to political science and dominant methodological approaches used hitherto by political scientists.

One of the leading scholars of black public opinion, Dawson does not compel survey researchers and public opinion scholars to rethink (or even consider) many of the following problems inherent to empirical investigations of group consciousness among various race-sex groups, including question wording and response choices, model misspecification, and measurement error in the independent variable. Arguing that models that fail to include all relevant variables will consistently lead to biased results that purportedly apply to all African Americans or women when political scientists fail to consider in-group variation between and among individual members of the group in question, I breach the wall between black feminist theorizing and mainstream political science by identifying ways in which public opinion scholars have ignored, conceptualized, measured, and modeled the intersection (or interaction) of race and gender consciousness. All in all, my book offers a great deal more by adding yet another voice to the debate surrounding black feminist sentiments, cross pressures, and the hierarchy of interests within the black community with an overriding purpose. Ultimately, I wish to show how the omission of black feminist voices causes survey researchers to ask the wrong

questions and base their empirical work and conclusions on unin-
terrogated assumptions—that, for instance, all of the women are
white, and all of the blacks are men.

No prior study has so broadly explored, using a national telephone survey sample of the adult African American population,
the extent to which black women and men support black feminist
tenets, or the simultaneous effects of race and gender on political
attitudes. Empirical assessments of black feminist consciousness
are rare. Most national surveys of Americans do not include a
large enough sample of black respondents and most national surveys of African Americans lack the items necessary to construct a
full measure of black feminist consciousness. Thus, the analysis at
hand is the first comprehensive attempt in years to gauge black attitudes toward gender equality and feminist priorities via public
opinion data gathered by a national telephone survey.

Much of the data analyzed in this book come from the
1993–1994 NBPS, which is a unique study in that it contains questions that measure black feminist consciousness with multiple survey items. It was conducted between December 1993 and February
1994. Respondents were selected in two ways: (1) from a national
random digit dial sample or (2) randomly from a list of households
in black neighborhoods. The response rate was 65 percent, resulting in 1,206 black respondents, all of whom were eligible to vote.
A full description of the survey may be found in the codebook,
which was compiled by its principal investigators Michael Dawson, Ronald Brown, and James Jackson (1993). Additional data
come from the 1984–1988 National Black Election Studies
(NBES), which is a unique study in that it contains questions that
measure sex role socialization and the comparative influence of
women with multiple survey items at the core of a basic feminist
belief system. The 1984 NBES was conducted from late July
through November 6, 1984, with reinterviews that began immediately following the national election. The 1988 NBES was conducted from August through November 8, 1986, with reinterviews
that began immediately following the national election. Comprised
of 1,150 interviews of black citizens, the 1984–1988 NBES were
modeled after the University of Michigan's landmark National
Election Studies (NES). A full description of the surveys may be
found in the codebook, which was compiled by its principal inves-

tigators Katherine Tate, Ronald E. Brown, Shirley J. Hatchett, and James S. Jackson.

Given that my objective is to chart a course for black women's studies in political science, I challenge the ways in which political scientists have traditionally defined and conceptualized group consciousness as either race or gender consciousness. More specifically, I reject the singular approach that dominates the group consciousness literature in an effort to address the simultaneous effects of race and gender. I therefore define and conceptualize black feminist consciousness, drawing on the ideas and experiences of African American women as they have endured the racism of their white sisters and sexism of their black brothers. I examine intragroup differences because this practice has long been omitted from feminist scholarship and black politics research.

Building on prior research, I posit that black feminist consciousness arises from an understanding of intersecting patterns of discrimination. Because the totality of black female experiences cannot be treated as the sum of separate parts, they must be analyzed together. If race and gender are studied as separate categories, one cannot explain how attitudes might change as a result of cross-pressures to subordinate the interests of black women so as to protect black men from racism. With this in mind, I start with a discussion of black feminist consciousness, providing a brief overview, offering a definition, and emphasizing themes that delineate its contours. To underscore the importance of studying black feminist consciousness and its determinants, I discuss the limitations of available data and quantitative approaches used hitherto by political scientists, as well as omissions in feminist scholarship and black politics research. By so doing, the present study sets itself apart from the extant literature on specific strands of group consciousness in political science.

In Defense of Ourselves: Black Feminist Theorists

Since slavery's abolition and women's suffrage, the character of black women has been attacked and impugned repeatedly, stereotypes of black women have been promoted for political ends (e.g., the matriarch, the jezebel, and the welfare queen), and black women have been blamed for numerous social and political ills (Davis 1981; Jewell 1993; Roberts 1997). Feeling called on to defend black womanhood and reject a plethora of cultural images that support stereotypes about intelligence and innate ability, black feminists from Anna Julia Cooper and Ida B. Wells-Barnett through bell hooks and Patricia J. Williams have explored the related ideas of "dual consciousness," of writing "from the borders," of theorizing as an "outsider" making creative use of their marginal status as "seventh sons" or "outsiders" with unreconciled strivings and warring ideals (W. DuBois 1994, 2). Black feminist theorizing then constitutes a pragmatic response to those circumstances that impinge the lives of black women (James and Busia 1993; Collins 1998, 2000; P. Williams 1991). For black female intellectuals who produce such independent specialized knowledge, the "outsider status is a kind of unresolved wound," whereby the burden of race and gender discrimination almost ensures the rejection of their intellectual work on epistemological grounds by a more powerful insider community (P. Williams 1991, 89). This sort of rejection is due to their lack of control over the apparatuses of society that sustain ideological hegemony and make the articulation of a self-defined standpoint difficult (Collins 1998, 2000).

In this sense, the present study can be added to a relatively short list of scholarly work that poses a fundamental challenge to the paradigmatic thought of a more powerful insider community. By demonstrating that the dominant conceptualization of group consciousness has been ineffective in articulating the politicized group consciousness of black women, this analysis urges public opinion scholars and survey researchers to reconsider the ways in which social scientists traditionally measure specific strands of group consciousness. It is argued here that black female intellectuals in particular, and black women in general, readily recognize disadvantage and discrimination due to their "dual identity" and their "politicized group consciousness" stemming from day-to-day encounters with race and gender oppression. The idea is that interlocking systems of oppression (racism and sexism) predispose black women to double consciousness. This notion of double consciousness connotes an acute sense of awareness.

Black women begin to see themselves through the eyes of others and measure their self-worth by the tape of a hegemonic society that expresses contempt for cultural images that promote negative stereotypes of black women for political ends (W. DuBois 1994, 2). Given that black women face discrimination on the basis of race and gender, it is likely that many black women possess a sense of group consciousness derived from their unique disadvantaged status in the United States. Similarly, it is quite possible that many black men are cognizant of and sympathetic toward the particular predicament of black women because they suffer from race oppression and class exploitation in the occupationally segregated labor market (M. King 1975; Stone 1979; D. King 1988). Thus, black women and men share a common experience that makes their individual fate inextricably tied to the race as a whole (Davis 1981; Jaynes and Williams 1989; Dawson 1994).

Defining Black Feminist Consciousness

Any discussion of black feminist consciousness must begin with some sort of definition, based on the literature derived from the ideas and experiences of black women. Many black academics, feminist scholars, and grassroots activists argue that African American women are status deprived because they face discrimination on the basis of race and gender. Having to bear the burdens of prejudice that challenge people of color, in addition to the various forms of subjugation that hinder women, African American women are doubly disadvantaged in the social, economic, and political structure of the United States. African American women occupy the lower stratum of the social hierarchy, are predominately found in clerical and service jobs, and are most likely to be single heads of households (Malveaux 1990; Rothenberg 1995; Rowe and Jeffries 1996; Smith and Horton 1997; Browne 1999). African American women also lag behind other race-sex groups on practically every measure of socioeconomic well-being: income, employment, and education. As a result, they are subject to multiple burdens—joblessness and domestic violence, teen pregnancy and illiteracy, poverty and malnutrition—which define their cumulative experience with race and gender oppression in the United States.

Much of the important work on black feminism comes from a small cadre of black female intellectuals outside of political science. The work of Audre Lorde (1984), Paula Giddings (1984), bell hooks (1984, 1989), Barbara Smith (1995), and Patricia Hill Collins (1990, 2000), among others, is both theoretical and qualitative. While these scholars provide a range of perspectives, several recurring themes that delineate the contours of black feminist thought appear in their work. I discuss the most salient themes in the following section.

First, black feminist scholars have focused on the concept of intersectionality. This is the notion that "race, class, gender, and sexuality are co-dependent variables that cannot be separated or ranked in scholarship, political practice, or in lived experience" when classism and heterosexism constitute twin barriers linked with racism and sexism (Ransby 2000, 1218). For this reason, Tamara Jones (2000, 56) reminds us that African American women "don't have the luxury of choosing to fight only one battle" because they contend with multiple burdens. Similarly, Adrien Wing (1997) argues that the actuality of layered experiences cannot be treated as separate or distinct parts when interlocking systems of oppression uphold and sustain each other in contemporary American society. Second, black feminist scholars have addressed the issue of gender inequality within the black community (Collins 2000; Harris 1999; hooks 1984, 1989; B. Smith 1995; Smooth and Tucker 1999). During the civil rights movement, black women were not recognized for their numerous political activities, such as behind-the-scenes organizing, mobilizing, and fund-raising (Payne 1995; Robnett 1997). Positions of leadership were reserved for black males. Wendy Smooth and Tamelyn Tucker (1999), who cite the Million Man March as yet another classic example, argue that in more recent years black women's activism has been ignored and black men have been given credit. Other scholars charge that the black church has validated the patriarchal nature of black male–female relationships through its biblical teachings and exclusion of black women from the clergy, key decision-making processes, and financial governing boards (Stone 1979; Higginbotham 1993; Harris 1999). Thus, black feminists recognize that gender inequality exists within the black community and point to the patriarchal nature of black male–female relationships within the context of the civil rights movement, the Million Man March, and the black church whereby leadership roles were reserved for black men (see, for example, Stone 1979; Harris 1999; Alexander-Floyd 2003).

Third, black feminists have maintained that feminism benefits the black community by challenging patriarchy as an institutionalized oppressive structure and advocating the building of coalitions. Black feminists have made conscious efforts to avoid attacking individual black men in order to work with them to further their cause of equality and justice for women. Collins (2000) maintains that black feminism is a social justice project and that building coalitions is central to advancing that project. Deborah Robinson (1987, 83) avers that the "black community must move from the position of singular activism for the good of the movement" because progressive black women are committed to struggle against both racism and sexism. In short, black feminism benefits the struggle for black liberation rather than divides members into factions because the fight against economic exploitation, gender subordination, racial discrimination, and heterosexism are intimately related to the pursuit of social justice (Ransby 2000).

Fourth, black feminists insist that a sense of belonging or conscious loyalty to the group in question (i.e., black women) arises from everyday experiences with race, class, and gender oppression (D. King 1988; Guy-Sheftall 1995). Shared experiences with interlocking systems of domination then drive black women and sympathizers to political activism (Robinson 1987; L. Williams 1987; Wilcox 1990, 1997). The individual who comes to realize that she shares a common fate with other black women, and that her individual life chances are inextricably tied to the group, begins to view collective action as a necessary form of resistance (Dawson 1994). Since the mid–1970s, black feminists and sympathizers have come to accept rallies, marches, and press conferences as necessary acts of resistance to Clarence Thomas's nomination to the Supreme Court, the exaltation of Mike Tyson upon his release from prison, and the Million Man March. This stage of group identification, whereby individuals see themselves as sharing a common fate with other black women, is referred to here as linked fate with black women.

Empirical Approaches

While the concept of black feminist consciousness is rich and well developed, empirical assessments of black feminist consciousness have been more limited. Political scientists have taken two main approaches to studying support for gender equality and feminist priorities among black women. First, scholars have used survey items for black women that were designed to tap feminist consciousness among white women. Both Pamela Conover (1988) and Elizabeth Cook (1989) have used this problematic approach to measure feminist consciousness. They assume that white feminism and black feminism are comparable. This is, in fact, an empirical question. A compelling body of literature suggests that there are many differences, both historically and in contemporary times, between the ways in which black women and white women experience sexism in this country. Thus, I argue that using survey items designed for white women results in a measurement of support for white feminism among black women—not black feminist consciousness. Second, political scientists have measured gender identification and race identification and then used the interaction of these two variables to create a measure of the politicized group identification of black women (Robinson 1987; Gay and Tate 1998). This measurement strategy is faulty because it assumes that race and gender identification are separate constructs. It has several problems, especially when considering that the hierarchy of interests within the black community prioritizes race over gender. For example, race identification became equated with an assertion of black masculinity during the black power movement with the rise of such nationalist organizations as the Nation of Islam and the Black Panther Party (Tate 1994). By prioritizing the lived experience of African American men and equating it with the black political agenda, the black power movement treated the struggle of black women against patriarchy as antithetical to the larger community narrative of racial discrimination. In light of this example, interaction terms composed of one measure of race identification and one measure of gender identification are far too simplistic. Ostensibly, this measurement approach fails to assess the simultaneity of oppression along with the hierarchy of interests within the black community.

Another limitation of the empirical research is its tendency to focus on feminist support among women without assessing the level of support for these same principles among men (Robinson 1987; Wilcox 1990; Gay and Tate 1998). Given the emphasis of many black feminists on building coalitions with black men and the rise of the men's movement to end patriarchy, it seems most appropriate to examine the extent to which black men endorse black feminist ideals. For this reason, I investigate the level of support for black feminist consciousness among African American women and men.

Arguably, the best measurement approach is one that captures the simultaneity of oppression with multiple items for various themes at the core of black feminist thought. This approach requires a model true to its theoretical origins, embracing several interrelated attitudes and beliefs derived from the ideas and experiences of African American women. The specification of basic models and the analysis of strategies employed must capture the core themes that define this unique angle of vision, arising from an understanding of interlocking systems of oppression. The project at hand addresses this need by presenting and evaluating a scale of black feminist thought, which is both reliable and internally coherent.

Overview of the Book

As Virginia Sapiro (2002, 21) puts it bluntly, "It's the context, situation, and question, stupid" that best illustrate problems inherent to theorizing about the relationship between gender and public opinion when using empirical survey research and polling data. For this reason, I begin each chapter with a leading black female activist in the context of (or amid) historical situations that precipitated her development of black feminist consciousness. Most of the African American women featured here have made vast contributions to the American political system, yet they have gone relatively unnoticed— Anna Julia Cooper, Ida B. Wells-Barnett, Sojourner Truth, Frances E. W. Harper, Maria W. Stewart, Mary Church Terrell, and Nannie Helen Burroughs. Each black female heroine sets up a fascinating puzzle, raises a stimulating question, or invites the reader to follow a line of argument. For example, the argument that I will make later in this book is that individual (or ascriptive) characteristics are less important than those factors rooted in lived experiences that make one ever so cognizant of interlocking systems of oppression. It is my view that objective conditions and concrete experiences warrant the development of black feminist consciousness—the ability to recognize that African American women face discrimination on the basis of race and gender.

African American women thereby provide the necessary background for a fuller appreciation of the claim that individual (or ascriptive) characteristics are less important than those factors rooted in lived experience, shining a light on material conditions and historical circumstances crucial to understanding multiple perspectives and realities as they relate to the unequal distribution of power and privilege in the United States. It is my hope that this approach might enable readers to critically evaluate American political processes, considering how our knowledge of the relationship between gender and public opinion might change if the history and experiences of these women were taken into consideration. Along the way, I will suggest that black women are not the only group who struggle with multiple group identities. It is quite possible for other race-sex groups to be cognizant of and sympathetic toward the particular predicament of African American women because they too suffer from race oppression, class exploitation, gender discrimination, and heterosexism in contemporary American society.

At the heart of this book are answers to the questions, How does the absence of black feminist voices impair our understanding of group consciousness? What factors make individuals more or less likely to adopt black feminist views? Are men just as likely as women to support black feminist tenets? Does black feminist consciousness lead black men and women to actively participate in American political processes? How important is black feminist consciousness relative to race consciousness in determining various modes of black political behavior? The analysis of survey data allows me to address critical questions that many black academics, intellectuals, and activists have devoted significant energy to debating without, to my knowledge, much empirical evidence that speaks to the normative components of the debate surrounding black feminist sentiments, cross pressures, and the hierarchy of interests within the black community. Social scientists, for the most part, have not investigated the simultaneity of oppression faced by black women or the core themes underlying black feminist consciousness using survey data and quantitative techniques. My overarching purpose is then to legitimize the study of African American women in politics through empirical survey-based research, which interrogates dominant approaches used hitherto by political scientists to measure either race or gender consciousness.

The following outline of this book offers a snapshot of the analysis to come in each chapter. Designed to direct attention to a variety of topics relevant to the book, it sets up an expectation in the reader's mind. The transparent narrative style makes the survey data and empirical analysis accessible to both undergraduate and graduate students. The book also serves as a resource for others doing similar empirically based research, regardless of methodology.

Chapter 2 provides a review of the literature, examining the range, scope, and content of extant literature on group consciousness. I start by answering two key questions that are directly related to the conceptualization of black feminist consciousness. First, how has the dominant conceptualization of group consciousness been ineffective in articulating the politicized identification of black women? Second, what have been the main approaches to studying the relationship between specific strands of group consciousness and political behavior? Along the way, I expose the deficiencies and limitations of dominant approaches that fail to consider the complexity of black female experiences: dual identity, cross-cutting versus consensus issues, and the hierarchy of interests. Unmasking problems inherent to research design and question wording, I argue that the choice of data to be analyzed and the interpretation of those data rest on a narrow and exclusive definition of group consciousness. No prior study has gone on to ask why, if this should be so, and clarify the findings when public opinion scholars and survey researchers traditionally measure race *or* feminist consciousness, not the intersection (or interaction) of these variables.

Chapter 3 provides evidence that black feminist consciousness is empirically distinct from race identification, and feminist identification. I begin by discussing the concept of black feminist consciousness and how it might be empirically measured. Using factor analysis, I examine whether the principal components of black feminist consciousness differ across gender. I then assess the level of support for black feminist consciousness, reporting the dimensionality of black feminist consciousness as it differs for black women and men when estimated separately. As it turns out, black men are equally and, in some cases, more likely to support black feminist tenets than black women.

Chapter 4 empirically tests various research hypotheses about the determinants of black feminist consciousness. Despite numerous studies of the determinants of feminist consciousness in the last decade, research on the determinants of black feminist consciousness has been far less common. Assuming that public opinion scholars and survey researchers are genuinely interested in how individuals adopt feminist views, social scientists must consider whether variables that predict one feminist perspective have a similar effect on another (Henley et al. 1998). The chapter takes up this task by (1) examining whether variables that affect feminist attitudes among white citizens have a similar effect on attitudes toward black feminism among African Americans and (2) considering whether the determinants of black feminist consciousness differ across gender among African Americans. More specifically, I investigate the effects of marital status, age, income, education, employment, religiosity, place of residence, interviewer sex, race identification, and power discontent on black feminist consciousness.

Chapter 5 empirically tests several research hypotheses about the overall impact of black feminist consciousness on various modes of black political participation. This chapter develops and tests a theory of the effect of black feminist consciousness along with demographic variables on black political participation. While few scholars have demonstrated the critical importance of black feminist consciousness as a determinant of political activism, even fewer scholars have investigated the simultaneous effects of race and gender consciousness on black political participation (notable exceptions being Robinson 1987; Wilcox 1990, 1997; Gay and Tate 1998). To date, the literature stops short of considering whether black feminist consciousness serves as an impetus for active participation in politics. By so doing, this chapter expands the standard socioeconomic model of black political participation to include black feminist consciousness.

Chapter 6 offers an interpretation of the results and concludes with a discussion of the research. Here, I set out to do three things. First, I review the findings of previous chapters and discuss their contribution to extant literature. Second, I assess the limitations of the data and methodology used here. Third, I consider what my findings mean for the future of feminist scholarship and black politics research. In the end, I make several recommendations.

I urge political scientists to design survey items that capture the simultaneity of oppression, privileging the lived experience of African American women so as not to silence black feminist voices. Otherwise, the study of public opinion and political behavior will remain largely limited with little prescriptive utility for individuals and groups that confront interlocking systems of oppression amid shifting political, historical, and material conditions. Of course, the move toward a more inclusive discipline with prescriptive relevance to marginalized groups can only be undertaken by those genuinely committed to social justice. My broadest goal is then to assist others in developing a framework within which to critically evaluate the American political system, disputing taken-for-granted views and considering black feminist perspectives that counter the mainstream.

As stated earlier, the book sets itself apart from previous empirical investigations of black feminist consciousness as it speaks to debates that exist both within and outside of political science. Following Mack Jones's (1977, 16) directive to "develop a political science which grows out of a black perspective" and abandon mainstream approaches, the book squares with an African American intellectual tradition derived from the "specialized knowledge" of a black woman's standpoint (see also Collins 2000, 34). All things considered, social scientists must begin to pay closer attention to in-group variation by controlling for confounding influences, considering the usefulness of alternative methodological approaches, and interrogating presumed group cohesion.

Chapter 2

FROM MARGIN TO CENTER
African American Women
and Black Feminist Theory

*True chivalry respects all womanhood. . . . Virtue knows no
color line, and the chivalry which depends upon complexion
of skin and texture of hair can command no honest respect.*

—Ida B. Wells, *On Lynchings*

On May 4, 1884, Ida B. Wells took a seat in the ladies' coach on a
Chesapeake and Ohio Railroad train en route to her teaching job in
Woodstock, Tennessee (Mulane 1993; Hine and Thompson 1998).
Since the 1875 Civil Rights Bill guaranteeing equal treatment in public accommodations had been repealed, the railroad was operating
under the "separate but equal" doctrine. Wells was therefore ordered
to leave the first-class accommodations in the ladies' coach for which
she had paid and move to the separate smoking car. When she refused, two conductors forcibly removed Wells from the train. In response, she sued the railroad and won her case. She was subsequently
awarded $500 in damages. Although the ruling was overturned by
the Tennessee Supreme Court three years later, she was the first black
person to initiate a legal challenge to the Supreme Court's nullifica-
tion of the 1875 Civil Rights Bill (Mulane 1993; Hine and Thompson 1998). This event and the struggles that followed it inspired
Wells to become a crusader for social justice and thereby marked a
turning point in her life—one that sparked a distinguished career
in journalism and active participation in public life. Thus, to fully
appreciate the historic significance of Ida B. Wells, it is necessary to

understand the degree to which her consciousness emerged out of and transformed everyday life experiences with interlocking systems of oppression into formidable acts of resistance.

An outspoken champion of women's suffrage and an ardent defender of black civil rights, Ida B. Wells decisively led a full-fledged movement for social justice credited with ending lynching in three states (Dawson 2001). During the last decade of the nineteenth century, she became internationally known for her protests against lynching via muckraking editorials, dynamic public speaking, and grassroots efforts that exposed the fraudulent claims used to justify these vigilante acts of violence against black people. More specifically, she developed a reputation for deconstructing the myth of the black rapist through painstaking investigative reporting, and tirelessly lobbying for antilynching legislation in the United States (James 1997; Hine and Thompson 1998; Dawson 2001). Both the radical nature of her message and her explosive style of delivery came under intense scrutiny and harsh criticism by conservative, black male leaders of the time—most notably, Booker T. Washington (James 1997; Schechter 1997; Hine and Thompson 1998; Dawson 2001). Wells's subject matter exposed the politics of "true manhood" and interpreted lynching as terrorism against black people in general and black men in particular. She broached a topic that was understood to be male terrain and, at the same time, directed critical attention to the assault of black women by white men for which no one was punished (Schechter 1997). While the aggressive style in which this message was delivered bore a striking resemblance to that of Frederick Douglass, the genius of Wells has since had to compete for intellectual dominance amid historical interpretations and theories of exceptional male genius as exemplified in the autobiographies of Douglass, which equate black liberation struggle with the assertion of black masculinity or manhood (S. Williams 1990; Carby 1997).

Douglass, who also opposed lynching and supported women's rights in his journalism, has been of continuing academic and popular interest in books and articles, as well as in the media (J. White 1985). Wells, on the other hand, has not garnered nearly as much attention when her theoretical analyses of race, gender, and patriarchal power linked black women's oppression through rape with black men's oppression through lynching without privileging one experience over the other (Carby 1997; Schechter 1997). In fact, she remains conspicuously absent from the canon on black civil rights from 1850 to 1920 that typically enshrines such legendary icons as Martin Delaney, Alexander Crummell, Frederick Douglass, T. Thomas Fortune, W. E. B. DuBois, Booker T. Washington, and Marcus Garvey who preceded the modern civil rights movement (see, for example, J. White 1985; Brotz 1992) and the canon on women's suffrage from 1848 to 1920 that typically enshrines such notable figures as Susan B. Anthony, Carrie Chapman Catt, Elizabeth Cady Stanton, Lucy Stone, and Lucretia Mott who preceded the contemporary women's liberation movement (see, for example, E. DuBois 1978; Evans 1989). This void in the literature presents an interesting puzzle, considering that Ida B. Wells fought on two fronts in defense of women's suffrage and black civil rights.

The contributions of Ida B. Wells cannot be overestimated. The written history of women's suffrage and black civil rights remains incomplete as long as she is not included in the historical record. Only within the last decade have academics, particularly black women historians, treated the diaries, letters, autobiographies, essays, interviews, and speeches of this remarkable woman as worthy of scholarly investigation. Still, she has not received proper recognition when her legacy has been misconstrued as counterfeminist by some and altogether dismissed by others (see, for example, Walker 1983; James 1997; Carby 1997). Thus, the life history of Ida B. Wells is emblematic of a larger problem: both the absence and the misrepresentation of African American women in black politics research and feminist scholarship.

Today, African American women follow in the footsteps of their foremothers—Anna Julia Cooper and Ida B. Wells—as they too remain either absent from the literature or misunderstood by political scientists. In light of this phenomenon, this chapter focuses on two key questions. First, how has the dominant conceptualization of group consciousness been ineffective in articulating the politicized group identification of black women? Second, what have been the dominant approaches to studying the relationship between specific strands of group consciousness and political behavior? To answer these questions, I assess the ways in which African American women have been theoretically erased from feminist scholarship and black politics research. Then, I examine the dominant approaches used hitherto by political scientists to measure race and gender consciousness that typically conceal the political orientations of black women. In conclusion, I argue that African American women respond to interlocking systems of oppression by integrating consciousness and political activism into their daily lives.

Group Consciousness:
The Study of Race *or* Gender, Not Both (?)

As stated earlier, black feminist consciousness is the recognition that black women are discriminated against on the basis of race *and* gender. This awareness of the simultaneity of oppression faced by African American women, however, is not captured by the dominant conceptualization of group consciousness, which tends to focus on *either* race *or* gender consciousness (Shingles 1981; Klein 1984; Gurin 1985; Conover 1988). By ignoring the fact that black women experience racism in ways different from black men and that black women have different experiences with sexism from those of white women, the group consciousness literature fails to address the unique situation of black women. Thus, the study of black feminist consciousness has been neglected—a troubling oversight considering the significance of group consciousness in determining political behavior (see, for example, Conover 1988; Gurin, Hatchett, and Jackson 1989; Dawson 1994; Tate 1994).

In 1972, Sidney Verba and Norman Nie identified group consciousness as a collective resource for African Americans because black respondents who frequently mentioned race in their discussion of politics were more actively engaged in politics than those who gave less race oriented responses and more likely to participate than white citizens within the same socioeconomic group. Arthur Miller et al. (1981, 495) refined this concept by arguing that group consciousness consisted of four components: group identification, power discontent, system blame, and collective action orientation. The first component, group identification, involves a "perceived self-location within a particular social stratum" accompanied by a sense of belonging or closeness (495). The second component, power discontent, reflects the recognition of and disenchantment with the status deprivation of the group in question. The third com-

ponent, system blame, connotes an awareness that structural barriers, rather than personal failings, account for the subordinate status
of the group. The fourth component, collective action orientation,
refers to a commitment to group strategies in confronting obstacles.

This refinement of the construct has led to subsequent research
using the same multidimensional model to measure specific strands
of group consciousness—specifically, race and gender consciousness.
The work of Richard Shingles (1981), Ethel Klein (1984), Patricia
Gurin (1985), Pamela Conover (1988), Elizabeth Cook (1989),
Clyde Wilcox (1990, 1997), Katherine Tate (1994), Michael C.
Dawson (1994), and Claudine Gay and Katherine Tate (1998) have
proven useful in assessing the implications of group consciousness
for public opinion and political behavior despite the limitations inherent to their methodological approaches. While I am critical of
this research, it must be noted that these scholars worked with data
sets not designed to measure black feminist consciousness and thus
were forced to rely on those items available to them.

The following section has been organized with a specific purpose in mind—one that is crucial to understanding the ways in
which African American women and black feminist theory might
be fully integrated into the discipline. As a scholar who is interested
in charting a course for black women's studies in political science,
I feel it necessary to evaluate and compare one methodological
approach after another in a critical way so as to emphasize the
ways in which public opinion scholars and survey researchers have
traditionally conceptualized and operationalized gender and race
consciousness as separate constructs. It is an issue of both practical
and theoretical importance for social scientists in general and political scientists in particular with interests in women and politics,
feminist theory, black politics, public opinion, and survey research.
More specifically, the organization of this chapter will prove helpful to scholars when they must prepare or evaluate research in the
above fields. From this point on, understanding that African American women have been theoretically erased from the literature on
gender and race consciousness is essential. Here, I argue that the
choice of data that have been analyzed and the interpretation of
that data rest on a narrow and exclusive definition of group consciousness, which effectively conceals the political orientations of
African American women.

Gender (or Feminist) Consciousness

Contemporary feminist scholarship has focused on the women's liberation movement and its ability to create strong bonds, raise awareness, and link consciousness to political activism among potential and active members. Relying heavily on data from the National Election Studies, this research often fails to recognize how the use of specific survey items does not capture unique aspects of black family life, the everyday experiences of African American women, collective action strategies, and issue priorities as they differ between black and white women. None of these surveys tap attitudes toward issues that disproportionately affect black women (e.g., protection from sterilization abuse). Nearly all of the research that has compared black and white women in national surveys lacks a large enough sample of African American women. Jane Mansbridge and Katherine Tate (1992), for example, rely on data collected from four national surveys—Gallup 1986, 1987; Yankelovich Clancy Shulman 1989; and Princeton Survey Research Associates 1990—where the sample size for black women ranges from 99 to 291 and the sample size for white women ranges from 876 to 1,868.

Arguing that African American women are more supportive of gender equality, feminist priorities, and the women's movement than white women, Mansbridge and Tate (1992) draw on hooks (1981) and Klein (1987) for supporting evidence. Citing data from a Louis Harris Virginia Slims poll conducted in 1972, hooks (1981) shows that African American women were more supportive of feminist ideology and more sympathetic toward women's liberation groups than white women. At the same time, she contends that many African American women rejected the women's movement because of its failure to address issues relevant to all women. Klein, who cites data from a Virginia Slims American Women's Poll conducted in 1985, shows that African American women were most supportive of the Equal Rights Amendment. Like hooks, she makes the argument that "adherence to ideology of sex equality is not synonymous with a sense of membership in the women's movement or an endorsement of all its policies" and considers black feminists and their work outside of mainstream feminist organizations as evidence for her claim (Klein 1987, 27). While most scholars agree that African American women are more supportive of gender equality and feminist priorities than white women, I disagree with those who maintain that African American women are more supportive of the women's movement than white women because our measures are deficient in several important ways.

Political scientists have used survey items for African American women that were designed to tap feminist consciousness among white women, relying on data that fail to problematize the group consciousness of African American women. As debates about intersecting patterns of discrimination abound outside of the discipline, few survey researchers and public opinion scholars draw on this growing body of literature to inform their empirical analysis of group consciousness. In practice, this has meant that survey items speak to the experiences (or issue concerns) of primarily white middle-class women, rather than poor women or women of color. By ignoring the work outside of the discipline, political scientists fail to consider the "specialized knowledge created by African American women which clarifies a standpoint of and for Black women" derived from their experiences (Collins 1990, 22). Instead, these researchers assume that white feminism and black feminism are similar.

In "Measuring Feminist Consciousness," Cook (1989) combined the feeling thermometer rating for the women's liberation movement with the "close to women" item in an effort to tap this specific strand of group consciousness among women. In her analysis, women who do not express closeness to other women are coded as lacking gender consciousness. Those who feel close to women, but rate the women's movement 50 degrees or less, are coded as having low consciousness. Those who feel close to women and rate the women's movement 51 degrees or more are coded as having high consciousness. In this instance, Cook overlooked the full array of factors that thwarted a formidable interracial women's alliance and led black women to organize around their own interests.

During its history, the women's movement reflected white middle-class bias in its objectives and aims (Fulenwider 1980; hooks 1981; A. Davis 1984). Its membership and leadership treated the interests of black women as secondary to their own by excluding them from the movement's agenda. Even today, these factors would likely influence the feeling thermometer rating for the women's liberation movement by black women. In fact, Claire Fulenwider (1980) documented a rising trend on the part of African American women that indicated lack of support for the women's movement and its tactics. While African American women were more supportive of feminist items that tapped perceptions of role socialization, sex discrimination, and the comparative influence of women versus men in society, they were far less supportive of those items that measured attitudes toward abortion and tactics for social change (Fulenwider 1980). More specifically, African American women, to a greater extent than white women, opposed the women's liberation movement, the belief that women need to organize and work together to combat discrimination, and abortion.

Using a measurement approach similar to Cook's (1987, 1989), Conover (1988) drew insight from a "woman's centered" perspective and focused on the extent to which women consciously identified themselves as homemakers. She combined the feeling thermometer rating for feminists with the homemaker item in order to measure feminist identity. The homemaker item specifically asked whether the respondent thought of herself as a "homemaker" most of the time, some of the time, occasionally, or never. Conover then examined the relationship between feminist identity and other criterion variables (i.e., feeling thermometer ratings for women, the women's movement, and the women's liberation movement) in order to establish measurement validity. In this instance, Conover overlooked the fact that the traditional housewife model has never fit most African American women (see also M. King 1975; Stone 1979; D. King 1988; Guy-Sheftall 1995; Collins 2000). African American women are more likely to be heads of households, historically their labor participation rate has exceeded that of white women, and they usually possess more decision-making authority in their parental and conjugal roles (M. King 1975; Stone 1979; D. King 1988; Prestage 1991; Guy-Sheftall 1995). Without much choice in the matter, African American women have worked at higher rates than white women because their families are burdened by family-income inequality and two incomes are necessary for familial economic survival. Even today, these factors would likely influence responses to the homemaker item by African American women. There are also additional factors that have gone unexplored.

Historically, African American women have felt called on to choose between their commitments to antiracist and antisexist struggles because the interests served by both have been cast as diametrically opposed (Robinson 1987). This conflict of interests has manifested itself around struggles for gender equality and feminist priorities, racial uplift, and black empowerment. Consider the Anita Hill/Clarence Thomas episode, an example of a struggle around gender equality and feminist priorities; this high stakes dispute between a black female law professor and a black male Supreme Court nominee called into question race loyalty for African Americans in general and African American women in particular. Still, the overwhelming majority of African American men and women expressed disbelief in Anita Hill's sexual harassment charges against Thomas (Mansbridge and Tate 1992). In light of this, Mansbridge and Tate (1992, 488–489) have argued that "the public image of a Black woman attacking a Black man" worked in Thomas's favor because "black women are often told to choose between race and gender, and often feel they must choose race" for fear they might be viewed as disloyal to the race.

Consider also the dissension around the Million Man March, an example of a struggle around racial uplift and black empowerment; this day of absence called on black men to assemble in the nation's capital for atonement. Writing in 1999, Smooth and Tucker contended that many black women "experienced inner conflict" as to whether they should support a "gender-exclusive call to march" on account of their dual identity as black and female (242, 251). This internal conflict is what Gay and Tate (1998, 183) have termed "doubly bound," which suggests that "black women will support their interests as women, but their support can be muted and even overwhelmed" when those interests collide with race. Ostensibly, the hierarchy of interests within the black community assigns priority to race over gender (Jordan 1997).

Race Consciousness (or Linked Fate)

Contemporary black politics research has focused on the political behavior of those African Americans who consciously identify themselves as members of an "oppressed group." Shingles (1981), for example, expanded the model of black political participation by demonstrating how mistrust, low political efficacy, and race consciousness related to heightened political participation among blacks. In his analysis, Shingles seemed to grasp the importance of intragroup differences by devoting scholarly attention to class differences in political orientations—the levels of political trust and internal political efficacy possessed by poor, working-class blacks versus middle-class blacks in relation to their rate of political participation. Yet, he failed to recognize the importance of gender via categorical analyses that concealed the political orientations and behavior of black women. Simply stated, black women were not studied apart from black men. This approach to the analysis of race consciousness and its effect on black political orientations and behavior guarantees that the uniqueness of black women and their "doubly bound" situation is ignored. With a few notable exceptions, very little work has looked at the political attitudes and behavior of African American women directly (notable exceptions being Darcy and Hadley 1988; Wilcox 1990, 1997; Gay and Tate 1998; Clawson and Clark 2003).

Few books have since raised immediate questions about gender differences in black public opinion and political behavior. Of those that have, I must note in particular: *From Protest to Politics: The New Black Voters in American Elections* (1994) by Katherine Tate, *Behind the Mule: Race and Class in African-American Politics* (1994) by Michael C. Dawson, and *Something Within: Religion in African-American Political Activism* (1999) by Frederick C. Harris. They offer highly sophisticated and comprehensive explanatory models of black political behavior, which place African American political thought at the center of their empirical analysis. Despite the valuable information they provide, these studies often fail to recognize the importance of theorizing gender.

Relying heavily on survey data from the 1984–1988 and 1996 National Black Election Studies, scholars have typically added the variable (gender) to a regression model and controlled for its effects statistically. By so doing, political scientists isolate the effects of gender from the influence of such confounding variables as age, education, and income. In this instance, gender is simply defined as whether a person is male or female and most often used to predict party identification, evaluation of particular candidates, and attitudes toward specific policy issues. This is not sufficient, especially when the categories of race and gender have been purposely deconstructed by feminists in general and black feminists in particular to avoid generalizations that purportedly apply to all women or people of color. A daunting task for researchers is then to work through the many questions surrounding these two categories by expanding our knowledge base of African American women's traditional political activity: voting and electoral behavior; the general characteristics of African American women active in political parties, including the significance of education, social class, and professional or occupational backgrounds; patterns of political recruitment and elite membership at the elective, appointed, and bureaucratic levels; and the factors that facilitate their entry into the political arena (Harmon-Martin 1994). Black political participation must be determined, in part, by an appreciation of the lived experience and policy objectives of African American men *and* women, especially when considering black feminist organizations have long been active in the policymaking process, specializing in research, policy analysis, litigation, and constituency development (Springer 1997; Ransby 2000). Protest activities, lobbying, monitoring public policy implementation, coalition formation, and campaigning are all strategies that have been used by black feminist organizations. Of course, the most useful approach to the study of African American women in politics would be one that privileges their ideas and experiences versus comparative analyses with other race-sex groups that report aggregate differences on the basis of race and gender defined as purely biological traits. This would mean also considering the cultural and social expectations prescribed by contemporary American society.

Theorizing Race and Gender

W. E. B. DuBois's work on the construction of race is applicable to the study of black feminist consciousness. His theorizing of double consciousness, as it has already been defined, contributes to our practical and theoretical understanding of the simultaneity of oppression. DuBois in particular had to balance his northern birth, the socioeconomic status of his family, and the fairness of his complexion against the suspicions of blacks and whites alike who occasionally questioned his ability to articulate the black experience authentically. His work was based on lived experience—his experience as a light-skinned, self-identified African American male in the United States. In fact, DuBois named his key text an "autobiography" of race because he felt strongly that the peculiar situations and problems of his people could best be explained in the life history of one who lived them (Sundquist 1996, 6).

Although DuBois sometimes spoke of race in biological terms, he resisted the notion that there were large fundamental differences between the races. As DuBois defined it, "[Race] is a vast family of human beings, generally of common blood and language, always of common history, traditions and impulses, who are both voluntarily and involuntarily striving together for the accomplishment of certain more or less vividly conceived ideas of life" (Sundquist 1996, 39). Not only was DuBois conscious of his blackness, but also he was conscious of the system in which blackness was socially constructed and transformed into products of human activity—performative gestures and excitable speeches that provided the illusion of an abiding racialized self. Assuming that the body is the site on which race is socially constructed and that blackness is an act that is constantly being done, DuBois's theory of double consciousness suggests that race becomes naturalized in the same way Judith Butler (1988) speaks of the naturalization of gender through the stylized repetition of acts.

According to Bulter, "The body is of necessity, a mode of embodying, and the 'what' that it embodies is possibilities. . . . The body is a historical situation . . . and is a manner of doing, dramatizing, and reproducing a historical situation" (1988, 521). Butler resists the notion of gender as an innate ontological trait. Instead, she categorizes the body as a historical situation as opposed to a natural fact. Gender is not a concrete identity, but an identity tenuously situated in time and instituted through a stylized repetition of acts (519). These acts conform to an expected gender identity shaped by society. "If gender is instituted through acts which are internally discontinuous," Butler suggests, "the appearance of substance is precisely that, a constituted identity, a performative accomplishment which the mundane social audience, including the actors themselves, come to believe and to perform in the mode of belief" (520). Assuming the body is the site on which gender is socially constructed and gender is an act that is constantly being done, Butler's theory of the naturalization of gender relates to DuBois's theory of double consciousness in several important ways.

These two theorists, DuBois and Butler, suggest that no matter how race and gender get mapped onto our bodies—whether it is the result of our cultural orientation, phenotype, or self-identification—these categories carry with them the history of the groups they represent. Like DuBois's theory of double consciousness, which forces the reader to consider the peculiar sensation that accompanies seeing oneself through the eyes of others always conscious of blackness, Butler's explanation of gender naturalization reveals the doubling of identity: the difference between being oneself and performing oneself. Everyday life experiences produce cultural performances and staged dramas that allow for some social input in the construction of character. The social drama created out of a real-life experience with race and gender discrimination constitutes a crisis or divisive outcome that the victim continues to work through after having the time and distance for reflective thinking. The original experience then creates an opportunity for working through similar episodes that become part of the fabric of a hegemonic society. Each episode is inextricably tied to the ways in which our identities get mapped onto our bodies as we relate to and interact with others.

For instance, African American women have long been aware of the levels at which male privilege and white privilege operate to erase black women's lives and perspectives. However, the need to subordinate matters of vital concern to these women for the sake of protecting black men from the forces of racism has taken precedence. Critical to understanding this phenomenon is the premise of Cathy Cohen's (1999) book. In *Boundaries of Blackness*, she argues that a linked fate framework treats crosscutting issues that affect subpopulations within the black community as either secondary or antithetical to those consensus issues reflective of the larger community narrative. Race identification acts as a primal lens through which crosscutting issues are evaluated in relationship to the hierarchy of interests, which prioritizes race over gender in the black community. Perhaps political messages that stress racial

equality and social justice by black activists and public intellectuals in the news media might shed further light on this point. The
interest in the discrimination experienced by African American
men in this country remains the most prominent issue on the black
political agenda today. Racial bias in the criminal justice system
has resulted in higher rates of incarceration for black men, and this
issue is viewed as more pressing than higher rates of poverty for
black female heads of households. In this instance, the struggle of
black women against patriarchy is secondary to the larger community narrative of racial discrimination, which equates black
male experiences with black liberation struggle. This relationship
between the black community and the interests of its female members is well understood and creates a powerful dynamic, especially
when some African Americans hold the view that feminism is the
cultural property of white women and that black women who
identify with it are less authentically black (Guy-Sheftall 1995;
Collins 1996; Jordan 1997). African American women, who are
told to choose between race and gender, often feel that they must
choose race to avoid being labeled as a traitor to the race. This
dilemma of having to choose between race and gender constitutes
a crisis or divisive outcome for black women.

Unfortunately, most empirically trained political scientists
who investigate aggregate gender differences in black public opinion and political behavior define gender in biological terms, how
men and women ought to behave politically, without exploring
varying ideas about masculinity and femininity or alternative kinds
of activities and characteristics that are appropriate for men and
women within the black community. For the most part, African
American women's public opinion and political behavior have
been measured against those of black men, white men and women,
or other women of color. For example, *From Protest to Politics:
The New Black Voters in American Elections* (1994) is marred by
a tendency to consider black men's political attitudes the norm
against which black women's political attitudes are measured and
found lacking. In her book, Tate avers, "Black women have
weaker racial identities than Black men" and speculates that black
women might form weaker racial identities because they are less
likely than black men to see themselves as victims of racial discrimination (29). Despite the fact that black women participated in

because this approach fails to consider difference between and among individual members of the black population. Given the salience of interlocking systems of oppression, as they circumscribe the lives of individual black women, African American women need and deserve their own items (Spelman 1988; Zinn and Dill 1996; Young 1997, 2000). Otherwise, the study of political attitudes and behavior will continue to conceal the political orientations of African-American women as they differ from African-American men and white women via categorical analysis that purportedly apply to all African Americans or women. For these reasons, the use of a single item to measure race identification should be avoided in survey research. Instead, I recommend the use of parallel items that ask, "Do you think what happens to [black women, black men] in this country will have something to do with what happens in your life?" By so doing, political scientists expand the traditional linked fate model to include items that assess in-group attachments.

The third text, Frederick Harris's *Something Within: Religion in African-American Political Activism* (1999), focuses explicitly on black female experiences as a point of departure for his analysis of the relationship between religiosity and support for gender equality within the black community. Harris argues that the black church has validated the patriarchal nature of male–female relationships through sermon and teaching of gender inequality. It is the case that "black women's exclusion from clerical leadership and key decision-making processes in their congregations" legitimizes black male authority and reinforces gender role stereotypes of black women as "doers" and "carriers" in charge of the private sphere (155). Harris finds that church attendance and active membership determine black women's support for gender equality. Black women who are most active in their churches are least supportive of the idea that African American women should share equally in the political leadership of the black community and are also least supportive of the notion that black churches or places of worship should allow more African American women to become members of the clergy.

Harris challenges conventional definitions of politics by adopting an approach that puts the perspectives and experiences of African American women at the center of his analysis. But at the same time, he casts male clergy as the model of leadership against

which women are found lacking authority when women are sometimes unable or unwilling to assume masculine postures. While he
devotes some attention to the obstacles to equality and empowerment for African American women, he falls short of making the
case for the feminist implications of his work by not compelling us
to consider how current black politics research might be changed
(or transformed) if the perspectives or lives of these women were
taken into consideration. If Harris wants to fully explore the correlation between African American women's participation in the
church and gender as a construct of theoretical importance, then
he must articulate how changes in these women's lives and activities reflect influence or perhaps destabilize patriarchal authority.
Identification of differences and commonalities among African
American women and men must also dispel false universalism,
which sets up African American men (in this case, clergy) as the
norm against which African American women appear to be deviant cases. While few scholars have focused as explicitly on the relationship between public and private domains as Harris has done
here, even fewer have offered empirical assessments of the simultaneous effects of race and gender.

The Intersection (or Interaction)
of Race and Gender

The dominant approach used to examine the intersection of race
and gender warrants further investigation. Political scientists have
measured gender identification and race identification and then
used an interaction term comprised of these two variables to measure black feminist consciousness. This methodological approach
is faulty because it does not capture the simultaneity of oppression.
Instead, it treats gender and race identity as separate constructs
and equates high levels of gender identity and race identity with
black feminist consciousness; just because a citizen has a strong
gender and race identity does not necessarily mean that person will
recognize the unique situation faced by African American women.
    Given that black feminist consciousness is a concept that em-
phasizes the simultaneous effects of race and gender, black respondents should be asked to consider both constructs simultaneously

when patterns of discrimination intersect in the lives of black women. African American women do not have the luxury of choosing to fight only one battle when interlocking systems of oppression uphold and sustain each other. Interaction terms composed of one measure of race identification and one measure of gender identification are far too simplistic. The totality of black female experiences cannot be reduced to an addition or multiplication problem. If race and gender are treated as separate constructs, there can be no account of how attitudes change as a result of cross-pressures to subordinate the interests of black women for the sake of protecting black men from racism. Moreover, interaction terms offer no means of measuring both commitment and belief toward the underlying themes that delineate the contours of black feminist consciousness.

While I am critical of this methodological approach, I would like to acknowledge that such studies provide important insights despite their limitations. Public opinion scholars and survey researchers have used interaction terms to determine whether race and gender are mutually reinforcing and predictive of such dependent variables as attitudes toward public policy, evaluations of notable black figures, and various components of race consciousness (see, for example, Robinson 1987; Gay and Tate 1998). Evaluating these studies on their own merits, I proceed with an in-depth discussion of two examples of interactive analyses of the joint effects of race and gender identities on African American women's public opinion and political behavior.

Using data from the 1984 National Black Election Study (NBES), Robinson (1987) tested two competing hypotheses about the effects of multiple group identity on race consciousness. One hypothesis suggests that black women who identify with blacks and women will possess a weaker sense of race consciousness than black women who identify solely with blacks. The other suggests that black women who identify with blacks and women will possess a stronger sense of race consciousness than black women who identify solely with blacks. In her analysis, Robinson constructs an interaction term that is the product of women's linked fate and black linked fate to measure multiple group identity. Demonstrating that those black women who identified with both their race and their gender possessed a stronger sense of race consciousness than those black women who identified solely with their race, Robinson concluded that gender identification among black women did not detract from race consciousness. Those black women who identified with their race and gender expressed a greater sense of power discontent and attributed the lack of group resources to societal barriers rather than personal failings. In this instance, multiple group identity differentially influenced the underlying dimensions of race consciousness by having a positive effect on power discontent and system blame. Robinson refutes the claims of those who maintain that an emphasis on gender divides the black community and undermines black male leadership with empirical evidence.

Using data from the 1984–1988 and 1996 NBES, Gay and Tate (1998) test two hypotheses about the simultaneous effects of gender and race on liberal policy positions. One hypothesis suggests that gender identification among black women will enhance the probability of support for liberal public policies. The other suggests that gender identification among black women will enhance the effect of race identification on support for liberal public policies. Like Robinson, Gay and Tate created an interaction term that is the product of women's linked fate and black linked fate. Although these two measures of race and gender identification are highly correlated, they can say with some degree of certainty that gender identification appears to enhance the effect of race identification on five policy issues: busing for integration, affirmative action, food stamps spending, spending on schools, and Medicare spending.

These examples constitute empirical investigations of competing hypotheses surrounding dual identity that advance our efforts to measure the simultaneous effects of race and gender. Both investigations found a positive relationship between race and gender consciousness using an interaction term (Robinson 1987; Gay and Tate 1998). The existing evidence supports the proposition that black feminist consciousness is intertwined with race consciousness; however, as discussed earlier, I argue that these researchers did not use the best measure of black feminist consciousness. Consequently, the jury is still out regarding the relationship between the intersection of race and gender identities. Also, these researchers limit their examination to an analysis of African American women without assessing support for these same constructs among African American men. While some readers may be skeptical that African American men can be black feminists, I argue quite emphatically that black feminist consciousness stems from the *recognition* that African American women are discriminated against on the basis of race and gender. In other words, black feminism is about ideology, not biology (Collins 2000; Dawson 2001).

Conclusion

This chapter began with a discussion of Ida B. Wells, which provided context for the theoretical argument presented here. Using a historic moment in the life of Wells as a starting point to critique feminist scholarship and black politics research, this chapter treated debates about the intersection of race and gender as historically situated knowledge virtually untapped by political scientists. Thus, I argued that efforts to examine race and gender must be understood in historical context and that a fundamental element of this historical context is the consciousness-raising success of both the black civil rights and the women's liberation movements. By drawing attention to the complexity of black female experiences and the tensions inherent to dual identity, I indicated just how difficult theorizing race and gender is for public opinion scholars and survey researchers. Contemporary scholarship on group consciousness has assessed implications for political behavior without careful consideration to African American women and the simultaneity of oppression. Through critical examination of the major works on race and gender consciousness, I exposed the deficiencies and limitations inherent to the extant literature in political science. By insisting that several methodological approaches to the study of race and gender consciousness have effectively concealed the political orientations of African American women, I challenged much of the scholarly work on group consciousness treating race and gender as separate, distinct categories.

Ignoring the ways in which group consciousness emerges out of and transforms everyday life experiences with interlocking systems of oppression into formidable acts of resistance is to mute black feminist voices and obscure the complexity of countless daily interactions. The first step in providing a more inclusive model of

African American women and black feminist theory is to expand our definition of group consciousness, acknowledge the differences that exist between and among various groups with multiple identities, and incorporate alternative models that address this diversity rather than attempting to fit all women or people of color into a general model. African American women's lives are complex, and our approach to understanding the intersection of race and gender should be equally complex. Public opinion scholars and survey researchers are then urged to guard against the tendency to use questions for black women that are designed with white middle-class women in mind. African American women, like other women of color, tend to have different experiences, needs, or problems. As a result, they are often treated differently from their white female and black male counterparts. Given that African American women are not the only group who struggle with multiple identities, it is my sincere hope that this book will persuade researchers to refine their conceptualization of group consciousness so that intersecting identities can be taken into account.

Perhaps in the years ahead, scholars will find race and gender no longer relevant variables. For now, however, the differences in the way men and women and whites and blacks are socialized to think about gender continues to influence American political processes. Thus, the exclusion of race and gender from our analyses impedes the development of black women's studies in political science.

Chapter 3

RACE TRUMPS
GENDER OR VICE VERSA?
Cross Pressures and Deliberate Choices

There is a great stir about colored men getting their rights, but not a word about colored women; and if colored men get their rights, and not colored women theirs, you see the colored men will be masters over the women, and it will be just as bad.

—Sojourner Truth, *History of Woman Suffrage*

When it was a question of race [I] let the lesser question of sex go. But the white women all go for sex, letting race occupy a minor position. . . . If the nation could handle only one question, [I] would not have the black women put a single straw in the way, if only the men of the race could obtain what they wanted.

—Frances E. W. Harper, *History of Woman Suffrage*

Shall we at this time justify the deprivation of the negro of the right to vote because some one else is deprived of that privilege? I hold that women as well as men have the right to vote, and my heart and my voice go with the movement to extend suffrage to woman. But that question rests upon another basis than that which our right rests.

—Frederick Douglass,
Frederick Douglass on Women's Rights

On February 27, 1869, the Fifteenth Amendment passed in the United States Congress. Prior to its passage, Frederick Douglass argued at a meeting of the Equal Rights Association that the ballot was "desirable" for women, but "vital" for black men because women were not as threatened by extreme acts of terror. As Douglass put it so bluntly, "When women because they are women are dragged from their houses and hung upon lamp-posts; when their children are torn from their arms, and their brains dashed upon the pavement; when they are objects of insult and outrage at every turn; when they are in danger of having their homes burnt down over their heads; when their children are not allowed to enter schools; then they will have the urgency to obtain the ballot" equal to that of black people in this country (Foner 1976, 32–33). Immediately following this speech, an observer in the audience pointed out that black women were victimized in the same way as just described. Douglass then insisted that black women were so treated on the basis of their race, not sex and that white middle-class women had ways to redress their grievances that were not afforded them (Huggins 1980). The logic behind this argument stressed that black women suffered from mostly the same problems as black men. Unwilling to accept Douglass's claim that it was the "Negro's hour" and that universal male suffrage must be secured first, the leadership of the women's suffrage movement and some of its members became openly hostile toward Douglass (Foner 1976; Huggins 1980; A. Davis 1981).

Both Susan B. Anthony and Elizabeth Cady Stanton felt slighted and argued that universal suffrage for women was no less compelling than universal male suffrage. These and other women suffragists who felt just as slighted expressed antiblack sentiment publicly and evolved into factions that eventually voted to disband the Equal Rights Association to form the National Woman's Suffrage Association. Given the role that women suffragists played in the abolitionist movement, they found it ironic that the vote would be granted to ignorant black male brutes over intelligent and refined white women. In fact, Stanton went so far as to proclaim that "it is better to be the slave of an educated white man, than of a degraded, ignorant black one" and to spearhead the movement to form the National Woman's Suffrage Association so as to separate herself from the cause of black people (Stanton et al. 1969, 94–95). Those women suffragists who did not feel so slighted believed that the Fifteenth Amendment, which granted universal male suffrage, regardless of "race, color, or previous condition of servitude," was a first step toward equal rights for women. Frances Dana Gage, a white middle-class woman suffragist, expressed this sentiment: "Could I with breath defeat the Fifteenth Amendment, I would not do it. That Amendment will let the colored men enter the wide portals of human rights. Keeping them out, suffering as now, would not let me in all the sooner" and thus found the positions of Anthony and Stanton whom she had supported for many years indefensible (Foner 1976, 36).

Of the few black women abolitionists who worked closely with white women suffragists, two public figures stood out and voiced their opinions. Frances E. W. Harper and Sojourner Truth expressed distinct viewpoints toward universal male suffrage. Harper, who sided with Douglass and supported passage of the Fifteenth Amendment, "let the lesser question of sex go" and observed that "white women all go for sex, letting race occupy a minor position" when the interests of black male abolitionists were pitted against the interests of white women suffragists (Stanton et al. 1969, 391–392). Conditioned not to see whiteness and its privileges, the leadership of the women's suffrage movement equated the experience of white middle-class women with the plight of all women and treated the interests of black women as either antithetical or secondary to their own (A. Davis 1981). For Harper, the propensity for white women suffragists to subordinate race in addition to their refusal to acknowledge the unique disadvantaged status of black women meant that woman suffrage was a whites-only affair in which she had no place. Outraged that white women suffragists would stand in the way of obtaining the vote for black men, Harper insisted that women—of any race—must take a step back and wait their turn so as not to jeopardize the political fate of black men (Hine and Thompson 1998, 157).

Truth, who opposed passage of the Fifteenth Amendment, did not side with Harper. That is not to say, however, that she supported the blatantly racist arguments put forth by Anthony and Stanton to secure the right to vote exclusively for white women (Yee 1992; Painter 1996; U. Taylor 1998). An acute observer, Truth recognized the patriarchal insistence of black male abolitionists to assert their right to vote over women of either race and the separate resolve of white women suffragists to assert their right to vote over black people of either sex. Truth, whose keen insight was ahead of her contemporaries, was not alone in understanding that black men abolitionists and white women suffragists effectively ignored the predicament of black women as differentiated social actors who also needed the vote. Understanding that racism and sexism constituted interlocking systems of oppression, many black women—most notably, Truth—continued to participate in the struggle to end slavery as well as the campaign to end patriarchy while maintaining their alliances with black male abolitionists and white women suffragists. By so doing, these women rejected the hierarchy of interests and refused to rank (or prioritize) their experiences with interlocking systems of oppression.

The struggle for the Fifteenth Amendment brings attention to the plight of black women, as they remain situated at the center of two distinct, yet related, movements and helps us understand the empirical analyses to follow in this chapter. Then as now, black feminist theorists argued that the hierarchy of interests within the black community assigns priority to race over gender. For this reason, today some black women (like Harper) subordinate issues of vital concern to them as women to protect black men (like Douglass) from racism and others (like Truth), when issues of race and gender collide, refuse to rank interlocking systems of oppression to protect their own interests as individuals who face twin barriers simultaneously. By refusing to prioritize race over gender, Truth gave birth to a radically different vision and sowed the seeds for contemporary black feminism today.

The Data

No prior study has explored the extent to which black women and men support black feminist tenets when cross-pressured to make deliberate choices about women's liberation and black civil rights using survey data and quantitative methods. The data analyzed in this chapter are from the 1993–1994 National Black Politics Study (NBPS) and the 1984–1988 NBES. The 1993–1994 NBPS is a unique study in that it contains questions that capture the simultaneity of oppression with survey items for various themes at the core of black feminist thought. Similarly, the 1984–1988 NBES is a unique study in that it contains questions that capture sex role socialization and the comparative influence of women with survey questions at the core of a basic feminist belief system. Considering that most national surveys of Americans do not include a large enough sample of black respondents and most national surveys of African Americans lack the items necessary to construct a full measure of either black feminist or feminist consciousness, such data sets are critical for more in-depth analysis of black attitudes toward gender equality and feminist priorities via public opinion data gathered by a national telephone survey of the adult African American population. Using data from the 1993–1994 NBPS and the 1984–1988 NBES, I develop and validate a measure of black feminist consciousness that is true to its theoretical origins. Along the way, I provide evidence that black feminist consciousness is empirically distinct from feminist identification and race identification. Finally, I assess whether the dimensionality of black feminist consciousness and the level of support for it differ across gender when black respondents are cross-pressured to make deliberate choices about women's liberation and black civil rights.

Measuring Black Feminist Consciousness

Since there is no one definitive measure of black feminist consciousness used in survey research with African American respondents, six items were selected from the 1993–1994 NBPS to construct this measure, reflecting four salient themes. The first theme is intersectionality, which suggests that interlocking systems of oppression circumscribe the lives of black women via day-to-day encounters with race, class, and gender oppression. It is measured by two survey items: the first question asked whether racism, poverty, and sexual discrimination were linked together and should be addressed by the black community (ADDRESS ALL DISCRIMINATION), and the second question asked whether black women suffered from both sexism within the black movement and racism within the women's movement (BOTH MOVEMENTS). The second theme is that gender (in) equality exists within the black community and beyond. It is also measured by two survey items: the first question asked whether black women should share equally in the political leadership of the black community (BLACK WOMEN LEADERSHIP), and the second question asked whether more women should become members of the clergy in black churches (MORE WOMEN CLERGY). The third theme is that black feminists benefit the black community by advancing the agenda of women. It is measured by one survey question that asked respondents whether black feminist groups help the community by advancing the position of black women or instead divide the community (FEMINIST HELP COMMUNITY). The fourth theme is linked fate with black women and involves the acceptance of the belief that individual life chances are inextricably tied to the group in question. It was also measured by one survey item that asked whether respondents thought what generally happens to black women in this country will have something to do with what happens in their own life (LINKED FATE WITH BLACK WOMEN). The same items were asked of black women and men. All items were rescaled to a 0 to 1 format with 1 indicating high black feminist consciousness. See Appendix A for complete question wording and response choices.

Data Analysis and Results

The first stage involved factor analysis delineating the principal components of black feminist consciousness. The goal of principal components analysis is to explain part of the variation in a set of observed variables on the basis of a few underlying dimensions. Here, we focus on explaining the total variation in positions taken by African American men and women on six items that arguably tap black feminist consciousness in an effort to determine the dimensionality of the common factor space. The principal components are ordered with respect to their variation so that the first few account for most of the variation in the original variables. Using this method, I determine whether all six items measure six different attitudes, one attitude, or something altogether different. I am also interested in whether all six questions are equally effective measures of black feminism.

Table 3.1 depicts the results of the exploratory principal components analysis for all six items. All items appear to load onto one

Table 3.1
Principal Predictive Factor (or Final Factor Solution) for Both Sexes

Survey Items	Factor 1: Black Feminist Consciousness
BLACK WOMEN LEADERSHIP Black women should share equally in the political leadership of the black community *or* black women should not undermine black male leadership.	.520
FEMINIST HELP COMMUNITY Black feminist groups help the black community by working to advance the position of black women *or* black feminist groups just divide the black community.	.509
ADDRESS ALL DISCRIMINATION The problems of racism, poverty, and sexual discrimination are all linked together and must be addressed by the black community *or* blacks should emphasize the struggle around race.	.588
MORE WOMEN CLERGY Black churches or places of worship should allow more women to become members of the clergy.	.467
LINKED FATE WITH BLACK WOMEN Do you think that what generally happens to black women in this country will have something to do with what happens in your life? Will it affect you a lot, some, or not very much?	.356
BOTH MOVEMENTS Black women have suffered from both sexism within the black movement and racism within the women's movement *or* black women mostly suffer from the same type of problems as black men.	.324

Source: 1993–1994 National Black Politics Study.

Note: For the "more women clergy" item, respondents were asked to indicate whether they strongly agree, somewhat agree, somewhat disagree, or strongly disagree with these statements.

principal predictive factor that accounts for 25 percent of the total variance, with an eigenvalue of 1.515. Notice that all of the factor loadings for the final factor solution are moderate to high, ranging from .324 for the "both movements" item to .588 for the "address all discrimination" item. The cutoff criterion used here is standard. Factor loadings less than .25 are not acceptable. While all six items are closely related and form an adequate scale for which to measure black feminist consciousness, they are not all equally effective measures of this construct. Considering that the "address all discrimination" item yields the highest factor score, the common factor space is likely driven by a sense that racism, sexism, and poverty are all linked together and must be addressed by the black community. Other scores within this range similarly suggest that black respondents recognize that black feminist groups help (versus divide) the black community by advancing the position of black women, support more women clergy at the pulpits of black churches, and believe that black women should share equally in the political leadership of the black community—all of which constitute hot button issues that black academics, public intellectuals, and grassroots activists have devoted significant energy to debating. Given that the "both movements" item yields the lowest factor score and the wording of the question invokes the hierarchy of interests, I run a factor analysis at a later stage for African American men and women separately to examine this result.

A long-standing debate exists within the black community about the relationship between black feminist consciousness and race loyalty (Guy-Sheftall 1995). Black civil rights organizations and their predominately male leadership have argued that feminism detracts from race loyalty and divides its membership into separate camps. From this perspective, a focus on sex discrimination inhibits, or even precludes, the development of racial awareness and black empowerment. Robert Staples (1970, 15–16) avers, "Any Movement that augments the sex-role antagonisms extant in the black community will only sow the seed of disunity and hinder the liberation struggle. Whether black women will participate in a female liberation movement is, of course, up to them. One, however, must be cognizant of the need to avoid a diffusion of energy devoted to the liberation struggle lest it dilute the over-all [sic] effectiveness of the movement." That is to say, the need to subordinate matters of vital concern to African American women for the sake of the civil rights movement should take precedence so as to protect black men from the forces of racism. Despite this position, many black feminist activists (e.g., Michelle Wallace, Ntozake Shange, Alice Walker, and Kimberle Crenshaw) have spoken out against sexism in their community to later find themselves criticized by black men and women who argued that airing "dirty laundry" only fed white efforts at racial domination. Still, black feminists maintain that interlocking systems of oppression (racism and sexism) must be addressed simultaneously as they are intimately related to the unequal distribution of power and privilege in the United States. Thus, it is consistent with the underpinnings of black feminist consciousness that feminist identification and race identification would be associated with it—at best, a positive relationship between black feminist consciousness, feminist identification, and race identification so as to suggest that black feminist consciousness is related to, yet distinct from, these two constructs.

I turned to other criterion variables that black feminist consciousness might be related to in order to test whether it is indeed a valid measure. Criterion-related validity (sometimes called predictive validity) is used to determine the extent to which a measure like black feminist consciousness is actually correlated to other distinct measures that it should be logically related—for example, feminist identification and race identification. In this instance, I examined the relationship between black feminist consciousness and feeling thermometer ratings for feminists and blacks as well as the feminist identification measure, which asked to what degree black female respondents support feminist ideals, and the race identification measure, which asked to what degree respondents felt that what happens to blacks in this country has something to do with what happens in their own life. Then, I examined the relationship between black feminist consciousness and an interaction term constructed from one measure of race identification and another measure of gender identification. Both items asked the respondent whether they felt what happens to [blacks and women] in this country will have something to do with what happens in their life. Table 3.2 depicts the results of this analysis. Correlation coefficients reflect the strength and direction of the relationship between variables and the degree to which one variable predicts another.

They range in value from -1 to $+1$. Correlation coefficients significant at the .05 level are marked with an asterisk, and those significant at the .01 level with two asterisks. Statistical significance indicates the likelihood that a relationship found in a probability sample exists in the population from which the sample was drawn.

While the relationship between black feminist consciousness and the feminist feeling thermometer is statistically significant, the two variables are weakly correlated. In addition, the relationship between black feminist consciousness and the feminist identification measure is weak and not statistically significant. Notice, however, that the relationship between the feminist feeling thermometer and the feminist identification measure is statistically significant and the correlation between these two variables is moderate, which suggests that a stronger relationship exists between these two measures of white feminism than with black feminist consciousness. My results bolster the claim that items designed to tap feminist identification among white women are problematic because they yield a measure-

Table 3.2
Correlations

	BFC	Feminists FT	Feminist ID	Blacks FT	Black ID	Interaction Term
Black Feminist Consciousness (BFC)	—					
Feminists Feeling Thermometer (FT)	.195**	—				
Feminist Identification (ID)	.056	.376**	—			
Blacks Feeling Thermometer (FT)	.077**	.178**	−.055	—		
Race Identification (ID)	.335**	.046	−.025	.096**	—	
Interaction Term	.366**	.097**	−.017	.083*	.876**	—

Source: 1993–1994 National Black Politics Study.

* = $p \leq .05$ (2-tailed); ** = $p \leq .01$ (2-tailed).

ment of support for white feminism among black women—not black feminist consciousness. Given that there are many differences, both historically and in contemporary times, between the ways in which black women and white women experience sexism in this country, it is fair to say that white feminism is related to, yet distinct from, black feminism.

I turn now to the relationship between black feminist consciousness, and the black feeling thermometer, and the race identification measure. Notice that the relationship between black feminist consciousness and the black feeling thermometer is statistically significant, but the correlation is weak. Similarly, the relationship between black feminist consciousness and the race identification measure is statistically significant and the correlation between these two variables is moderate. Likewise, the relationship between the feeling thermometer for blacks and the race identification measure is statistically significant. However, these two variables are weakly correlated. Most striking is the relationship between black feminist consciousness and the interaction term. In prior research, political scientists have measured gender identification and race identification and then used the interaction of those two variables to create a measure of black feminist consciousness (Robinson 1987; Gay and Tate 1998). This strategy treats gender and race identity as separate constructs and equates high levels of gender identity and race identity with black feminist consciousness. Here, the relationship between the interaction term and black feminist consciousness is statistically significant and the correlation is moderate. Considering that the interaction term assumes that race and gender are separate constructs and black feminist consciousness emphasizes the simultaneity of oppression, the results were fairly predictable. If black feminist consciousness were to have both a statistically significant relationship and moderate correlation with any one measure, it would be with the interaction term because it contains one measure of gender identification and one measure of race identification. In other words, the interaction term versus the feminist feeling thermometer and feminist identification measure as well as the black feeling thermometer and race identification measure represents the one measure that comes closest to capturing two components (gender identification and race identification) of black feminist consciousnesss.

In summary, the relationship between black feminist consciousness and respective feeling thermometers for feminists and blacks reached statistical significance. However, these variables were weakly correlated. While the relationship between black feminist consciousness and the feminist identification measure was not statistically significant, the relationship between black feminist consciousness and the race identification measure was statistically significant. Although black feminist consciousness and the feminist identification measure were weakly correlated, black feminist consciousness and the race identification measure were moderately correlated. Most striking was the relationship between black feminist consciousness and the interaction term because it was both statistically significant and moderately correlated. All things considered, the empirical findings cited here bolster my claim that black feminist consciousness is related to, yet distinct from, both feminist identification and race identification.

The second stage of analysis involved factor analysis delineating the principal components of black feminist consciousness for black women and men separately. It is believed that the "both movements" item may be more difficult for respondents to answer because this item in particular activates the sense of "internal conflict" invoked by the hierarchy of interests often experienced by black women and men when women's liberation is pitted against black civil rights. This "internal conflict" is what Gay and Tate (1998) have termed "doubly bound," which suggests that black women will support their interest as women, but their support can be muted or even overwhelmed when those interest collide with race (183). The "both movements" item captures this sense of "internal conflict" by forcing respondents to consider whether African American women suffer from both sexism within the black movement and racism within the women's movement or whether black women suffer from mostly the same problems as black men.

Table 3.3 depicts the results of this second stage of analysis for all six items, which appear to tap one clear underlying dimension of black feminist consciousness for black women. Notice that all the factor loadings for the final factor solution were relatively high, ranging from .396 for the "both movements" item to .610 for the "address all discrimination" item. With black men absent from this analysis, both factor scores rose slightly from before when both sexes were included in the model.

Table 3.3
Final Factor Solution for Black Women

	Black Feminist Consciousness
BLACK WOMEN LEADERSHIP	.438
FEMINIST HELP COMMUNITY	.432
ADDRESS ALL DISCRIMINATION	.610
MORE WOMEN CLERGY	.518
LINKED FATE WITH BLACK WOMEN	.565
BOTH MOVEMENTS	.396

Source: 1993–1994 National Black Politics Study.
Eigenvalues = 1.495   Variance = 25%.

Table 3.4 depicts the results of this second stage of analysis for all six items, which appear to tap two underlying dimensions of black feminist consciousness for black men. Notice that the first five factor loadings for the final factor solution were relatively high, ranging from .396 to .625. The "more women clergy" item is the lowest at .396 and the "black women leadership" item is the highest at .625. Notice also that the "both movements" item clearly determines the second dimension for black men. Given these results, I conclude that the "both movements" item is uncorrelated (or correlated more weakly) with the items that comprise the first dimension for black men. Instead, it appears to explain the second dimension.

The third stage of analysis involved cross-tabulation in an effort to determine whether the level of support for black feminist consciousness differs across gender. This method helped organize, describe, and summarize observations. For cross-tabulations, the independent variable (gender) represents the column variable (listed across the top), and the dependent variable (black feminist consciousness) represents the row variable (listed at the left side of the table). Whereas the computation of percentages goes down the columns, the comparison cuts across the rows. More specifically, the proportion of black women who possess black feminist consciousness was compared to the proportion of black men who support its fundamental tenets.

Table 3.4
Final Factor Solution for Black Men

	Black Feminist Consciousness	Hierarchy of Interests
BLACK WOMEN LEADERSHIP	.625	−.296
FEMINIST HELP COMMUNITY	.603	−.296
ADDRESS ALL DISCRIMINATION	.536	.133
MORE WOMEN CLERGY	.396	−.008
LINKED FATE WITH BLACK WOMEN	.596	.028
BOTH MOVEMENTS	.189	.942

Source: 1993–1994 National Black Politics Study.

Eigenvalues = 1.589; 1.013   Variance = 26%; 17%.

Table 3.5 presents the level of support for black feminism. It would appear that black feminist consciousness is quite widespread among black women and black men. Roughly 70 percent of all respondents believe that race and sex discrimination are linked together. Another 68 percent report that black feminist groups are beneficial to the black community because they advance the position of black women. An even greater proportion, 78 percent, endorse the notion that black women should share equally in the political leadership of the black community and express that what generally happens to black women in this country will have something to do with their own life. While there is less support for black female clergy, the majority, 55 percent indicates that more black women should be allowed to become members of the clergy.

The results of the aforementioned items alone suggest that black women and men recognize that the problems of racism, poverty, and sexual discrimination are all linked together; black feminists are beneficial to the black community; black women should share equally in the political leadership; black women should take on a more prominent role in the black church; and the overwhelming majority of respondents (black men and women) felt they share a common fate with black women. These findings also suggest that black men are equally and, in some cases, more

Table 3.5

Percent of Black Women and Men Who Take Black Feminist Position

	Black Women N=781	Black Men N=425	TOTAL N=1,206
The problems of racism, poverty, and sexual discrimination are all linked together. (ADDRESS ALL DISCRIMINATION)	71%	68%	70%
Black feminist groups help the black community by advancing the osition of black women. (FEMINIST HELP COMMUNITY)	69%	65%	68%
Black women should share equally in the political leadership of the black community. (BLACK WOMEN LEADERSHIP)	77%	79%	78%
Black churches or places of worship should allow more women to become members of the clergy. (MORE WOMEN CLERGY)			
Agree	54%	59%	55%
Strongly Agree	41%	53%	47%
What generally happens to black women in this country will have something to do with your life. (LINKED FATE WITH BLACK WOMEN)	70%	72%	71%
Black women have suffered from both sexism within the black movement and racism within the women's movement. (BOTH MOVEMENTS)	55%	49%	53%

Source: 1993–1994 National Black Politics Study.

Note: For the "more women clergy" item, the first table entry is the percentage of respondents who indicated that they strongly or somewhat agreed with that statement and the second table entry is the percentage of respondents who indicated that they strongly agreed with that statement. For the "linked fate" item, the table entry is the percentage of respondents who indicated that they thought what generally happens to black women will affect them a lot or some.

likely than black women to support black feminism. For instance, when we examine just those who "strongly agree" with the position that there should be more black women clergy, a twelve-point difference exists between black women and men. This finding is most interesting, especially when considering the history of the black church. It is no secret that the black church has played a pre-eminent role in inhibiting the development of black feminist consciousness (Stone 1979; Harris 1999).

Of course, an alternative explanation could be that black men are following in the footsteps of their forefather—Frederick Douglass. It is quite possible that many black men are cognizant of and sympathetic toward the particular predicament of black women; however, when women's liberation and black civil rights are pitted against each other, they too will prioritize race over gender and argue that black women suffer from mostly the same problems as black men. Both African American men and women suffer from race oppression and class exploitation in the occupationally segregated labor market. The income and earnings of African American men lag behind those of white men, which suggests that black men are subordinate to white men in the occupational structure of the United States (Gooding-Williams 1993; Wilson 1996; Browne 1999). Similarly, the income and earnings of black women lag behind those of white women, which suggests that black women are subordinate to white women in the occupational structure of the United States (Gooding-Williams 1993; Wilson 1996; Browne 1999). Together, they are burdened by poverty, lack of job skills, and wage inequality (Crenshaw 1993). Given their shared experience with race oppression and class exploitation, many black men might recognize that such twin barriers make their individual fates inextricably tied to the race as a whole (A. Davis 1981; Jaynes and Williams 1989; Dawson 1994). Identifying with black women as another marginalized group, black men are then willing to support the interests of black women as long as they do not perceivably jeopardize the movement for black civil rights.

Still, the black church is perhaps the most important social institution in the black community. It has validated the patriarchal nature of male–female relationships through sermon and teaching of gender inequality in addition to purposeful exclusion of black women from clerical leadership, key decision–making processes, and financial governing boards (Stone 1979; Harris 1999). While male-dominated groups such as the deacon and steward boards govern the church with formal authority and power in deciding church policy and financial matters, women-dominated groups such as the deaconess and stewardess boards govern with far less power and authority. These women-only groups manage Sunday schools, child day-care services, youth groups, and bake sales. Despite the fact that more women are becoming deacons and stewards today, these women continue to govern with less authority than their male counterparts in similar positions because sexism within the black church remains ever so prevalent (Harris 1999). As a result, black women have created alternative and separate religious spheres that enable them to assert some influence on decision-making processes despite resistance from male-dominated spheres (Higginbotham 1993; Harris 1999). In fact, some black women have begun to establish their own congregations and storefront churches. Still, many black women are not so disenchanted with black churches and fail to resist blatantly chauvinist attitudes when exhibited by their brothers and sisters in the church because they have come to accept positions that are secondary to black men as traditionally female. Conditioned not to see patriarchy, they willingly accept the most demeaning and uncreative service jobs so as not to undermine black male authority. Coincidently, black men are more than willing to relinquish power and control over those tasks they perceive to be menial and assign them to black women (e.g., Sunday schools, child day-care services, youth groups, and bake sales).

Nevertheless, the question that remains unanswered is whether black men have truly progressed in their thinking about traditional gender roles. In an effort to address this question, I explore whether these results (particularly the equal likelihood of black men advocating the black feminist agenda as women) reflect the type of questions asked more than the reality and, perhaps, the ingenuity of black men to respond with politically correct answers. Thus, I examine the responses to the "both movements" item, which arguably taps the sense of "internal conflict" experienced by black women and men when they feel they must choose race over gender. By openly addressing the hierarchy of interests within the black community that assigns priority to race over gender, this item in particular makes it more difficult for black men to uphold the black feminist position because they must consider whether black women experienced sexism within the black movement.

Presented in table 3.5, the majority of black women (55 percent) indicate that black women suffer from both sexism within the black movement and racism within the women's movement. By so doing, these women refuse to rank interlocking systems of oppression and reject the hierarchy of interests within the black community. Less than half of black men (49 percent) indicate that black women suffer from both sexism within the black movement and racism within the women's movement. Instead, the majority of black men (51 percent) report that black women suffer from mostly the same problems as black men. By so doing, these men refuse to air their "dirty laundry" and pledge loyalty to the race. It would appear on the basis of the analyses cited here that the "both movements" item activates the sense of "internal conflict" invoked by the hierarchy of interests when women's liberation is pitted against black civil rights, particularly for black men. While both African American men and women experience some sense of "internal conflict" invoked by the hierarchy of interests, it does not produce the same divisive outcome for black women as it does for black men. Of course, additional items would yield greater insight and provide more substantive answers to this question of whether black men have truly progressed in their thinking about traditional gender roles. While we look to alternative data for this answer, we might also find questions that mark a clear distinction between black women and men on these issues.

Using data from the 1984–1988 NBES, I found that there was a significant difference in the responses to three items by black women and men that might tell us a great deal more. One item asked respondents whether men were better suited emotionally for politics. Another asked whether [men and women] possess too much influence, just about the right amount of influence, or too little influence. Presented in table 3.6, the results of this analysis indicate that roughly 39 percent of black women strongly disagree with the statement that men are better suited for politics versus 27 percent of black men. And while less than half of the male respondents (45 percent) indicated that men have too much power, the majority of women (60 percent) indicated that men did in fact possess too much power. Finally, one-third of black women (30 percent) believed that women have far too little power, in contrast with less than one-quarter of black men (24 percent). While these items do not capture the full essence of black feminist thought, they do successfully capture some component of feminism. In prior research, scholars have used similar items that tapped perceptions of sex role socialization and the comparative influence of women in society. In fact, Fulenwider (1980, 44) identified such items as "basic to the core belief structure of a feminist belief system."

Using data from the 1972–1976 American National Election Studies, Fulenwider (1980) discovered a startling trend in minority attitudes toward feminism. In 1972, minority men were almost twice as likely as minority women to oppose feminism, but by 1976, the reverse became true. While 29 percent of minority women opposed feminism, only 13 percent of minority men opposed feminism. Item analysis revealed that minority women were more opposed to the women's liberation movement, when asked to

Table 3.6
Percent of Black Women and Men Who Take Feminist Position

	Black Women N=777	Black Men N=439	Total N=1,216
Men are better suited for politics.			
Disagree	59%	47%	53%
Strongly Disagree	39%	27%	33%
Men have too much influence.			
Agree	60%	45%	53%
Women have too little influence.			
Agree	66%	50%	59%
Women have far too little influence.			
Agree	30%	24%	27%

Source: 1984–1988 National Black Election Studies.

Note: The first item asked respondents whether they strongly agree, somewhat agree, somewhat disagree, or strongly disagree with the statement that men are better suited for politics. Other items asked whether [men and women] possess too much influence, just about the right amount of influence, or too little influence. Is that somewhat too little influence or far too little influence?

rate the movement according to a feeling thermometer, and its tactics for social change that involved women—of any race—organizing and working together. Given that the women's liberation movement reflected the aims and objectives of white middle-class women, its leadership treated the interests of black women as less important, and many black women organized separately around their own interests, this trend on the part of black women is not particularly surprising.

Using data from the 1993–1994 NBPS and the 1984–1988 NBES, I discovered a similar trend in attitudes toward gender equality and feminist priorities among African Americans. The fact that black men are equally and, in some cases, more likely to endorse black feminist tenets than black women lends support to the idea that the attitudes of African American women and men toward gender equality and feminist priorities changed over time. Of course, further analysis must be conducted to investigate this phenomenon in more detail.

Conclusion

The study of black feminist thought is an act charged with political significance because, at the very least, it means that black feminists have a voice and with this newfound voice comes an unquestionable dilemma (Collins 1996). Black feminists are situated at the center of two political movements that when cast as diametrically opposed create uneasy alliances. While both the women's suffrage and abolitionist movements initially supported collaborative efforts to build coalitions and actively participate in politics, loyalists were later forced to either choose or rank oppressions when faced with real-life circumstances that necessitated deliberate choices surrounding passage of the Fifteenth Amendment. Intense debates over universal male suffrage gave rise to competing agendas, complex misunderstandings, and dissimilar interpretations of the same monumental event for all parties involved—black male abolitionists, white women suffragists, and black women with joint alliances who were situated in the most precarious position (Guy-Sheftall 1995; Terborg-Penn 1998). For black women, who are the physical and material representation of the race-sex correspondence, the level of discomfort is never lost and the ability to adopt a dispassionate, objective stance toward crosscutting issues that so obviously affect them personally is virtually impossible. They are neither prepared to suffer publicly, through intense and passionate advocacy, nor willing to be dismissed, belittled, or rejected by other members of their race or sex for making the wrong decision. Most certainly related to their social location in the United States and their subordinate position within two marginalized groups, the hierarchy of interests defines the material conditions that bound their lives.

As shown by the factor analysis delineating the principal components of black feminist consciousness for both sexes, all six items appear to load onto one principal predictive factor. As shown by the factor analysis delineating the principal components of black feminist consciousness for black women, all six items again appear to load onto one principal predictive factor. However, as shown by the factor analysis delineating the principal components of black feminist consciousness for black men, a clearly different structure exists for them. The "both movements" item, which captures the sense of "internal conflict" invoked by the hierarchy of interests when women's liberation is pitted against black civil rights, clearly defines a second dimension to this construct.

While it would appear that black feminist consciousness is quite widespread among black women and men, black men in particular are equally and, in some cases, more likely to support black feminism with one exception—the "both movements" item—and when we examine just those who "strongly agree" with the position that there should be more black women clergy a twelve-point difference exists between black women and men. Given the history of the black church, this finding is particularly perplexing. Of course, an alternative explanation might be that black men so identify with black women that they recognize their unique disadvantaged status. Still, black churches have played a preeminent role in inhibiting the development of black feminist consciousness and, as a result, the question that remained unanswered is whether black men have truly progressed in their thinking of traditional gender roles (Stone 1979; Harris 1999). For this reason, I turned to another data set with more difficult questions that marked a distinction between black women and men. The purpose of this analysis was to determine whether the items available in the 1993–1994 NBPS failed to raise the bar high enough to truly separate those with a genuine commitment to black feminist principles from those with only a fleeting recognition of the discrimination faced by black women. Using data from the 1984–1988 NBES, I found that black women and men differ in their related beliefs toward sex role socialization and the comparative influence of women in society.

All things considered, it would appear on the basis of the principal components analysis cited here that black citizens' beliefs about equality for black women fall along one clear dimension: one of black feminist consciousness. This construct organizes the way black people think about political issues affecting the lives of black women. Although these items are quite diverse in that they address the problems of racism, poverty, and sexism, black feminism as a racially divisive issue, common fate as an advanced stage of group identification, gender equality within the black community as well as the black church, and an awareness that black women suffered from both sexism within the black movement and racism within the women's movement, responses to these questions are driven by the same sense of black feminist consciousness. Using data from the 1993–1994 NBPS and the 1984–1988 NBES, I conclude that black consciousness is a stable construct that shapes the beliefs of black women and men.

Chapter 4

BLACK FEMINIST CONSCIOUSNESS AND ITS DETERMINANTS
Factors Rooted in Experience

How long shall the fair daughters of Africa be compelled to bury their minds and talents beneath a load of iron pots and kettles? Until union, knowledge and love begin to flow among us. How long shall a mean set of men flatter us with their smiles, and enrich themselves with our hard earnings; their wives' fingers sparkling with rings, and they themselves laughing at our folly?

—Maria W. Stewart, *Women and Men Political Theorists: Enlightened Conversations*

In 1803, Maria W. Stewart was born in Hartford, Connecticut. Both of her parents, about whom little else is known except that they were African and freeborn, died by the time she was five years old (Sterling 1984; Richardson 1987; Waters 2000; Andrews 2003). From the time of their deaths until she was fifteen, Maria worked as a domestic servant for a local clergyman and his family. By the age of sixteen, she moved to Boston where she attended "Sabbath schools" and became well versed in religious doctrine and biblical teaching. While she took religious education classes, Maria supported herself as a domestic servant. In 1826, the twenty-three-year-old Maria married James W. Stewart who was a veteran of the War of 1812 and an independent businessman with a considerable amount of wealth (Sterling 1984; Andrews 2003). Three years after their marriage, he died. Unscrupulous lawyers then robbed Maria of the inheritance her husband provided, leaving her destitute. In the depths of despair and heartache, Maria was victimized by a group of white businessmen so intent on profiting from her husband's death that they produced a mystery woman who posed as a competing widow for the estate that James left his only wife: Maria W. Stewart. The loss of her husband and the struggles that followed inspired Maria to undergo a religious conversion whereby she professed her faith publicly and dedicated the remainder of her life to community service.

To fully appreciate the historic significance of Maria W. Stewart, it is necessary to understand the degree to which her religious conversion emerged out of and transformed everyday life experiences with interlocking systems of oppression into formidable acts of resistance that brought her religious vision and political agenda together on center stage before intrigued audiences (Richardson 1987; Hine and Thompson 1998; Waters 2000). Generally recognized as the first American-born woman to lecture in public, Maria spoke on behalf of women's liberation and black civil rights before paying audiences at a time when "Negro speakers" were virtually unknown and it was absolutely unheard of for women to address audiences that included men (Giddings 1984; Richardson 1987; Guy-Sheftall 1995; Hine and Thompson 1998; Collins 2000). In the years to come, when she became the target of negative reviews and slander, Stewart claimed that her authority to speak on some of the most controversial and vexing political issues of the nineteenth century—black liberation, women's suffrage, and black empowerment—were divinely sanctioned. In other words, she defended her right to speak on behalf of women's liberation and black civil rights, and then asserted her right to be heard before black and white audiences alike.

Evangelical in style, her speeches admonished black men for not doing enough for racial uplift, neglecting their duty to their families and communities, and exhibiting chauvinistic attitudes toward the women of their race (Giddings 1984; Hine and Thompson 1998). Her indictment of black male authority led to sharp criticism from conservative leaders who argued that she had overstepped her boundaries by augmenting sex-role antagonisms extant in the black community, which only fed white efforts at racial domination. Nonetheless, she called on her critics to develop racial pride and self-help strategies that would enhance educational and employment opportunities so as not to depend on white society to solve the problems of the race. Despite her endorsement of self-determination and economic independence, few academicians have come to recognize Maria W. Stewart as one of the first black nationalists. Instead, she goes down in history as a little known political writer whose unpopular speeches and actions led to her subsequent character assassination by both black and white civil society in the nineteenth century (Romero 1997; Hine and Thompson 1998; Collins 2000; Waters 2000).

By violating the taboo against women speaking before public audiences, Maria W. Stewart set the stage for others like Anna Julia Cooper, Ida B. Wells-Barnett, and Sojourner Truth to similarly overstep boundaries and broach topics that were considered exclusively male terrain. A daring and courageous public speaker, Stewart established a trend in political activism that has since lacked much critical assessment and analytical rigor today. For more than half a century, Stewart devoted her life to public service by joining women's organizations and literary societies, giving public lectures, and committing her thoughts to paper, as well as teaching at various academic institutions (Sterling 1984; Richardson 1987; Collins 2000; Waters 2000). While Maria W. Stewart might certainly be the first American-born woman to air her views on the platform, she surely is not the last to be condemned and ridiculed for speaking on behalf of women's liberation and black civil rights. Compared to Anna Julia Cooper, Ida B. Wells-Barnett, and Sojourner Truth—all of whom underwent some sort of "conversion" that resulted from their lived experience with interlocking systems of oppression and subsequently led to their active participation in public life—Maria W. Stewart represents the first among them to "feel the iron" when serious structural barriers were in place to prevent women from entering the political arena.

Undeterred by cultural norms that forbade women of any race to raise political issues in a public forum, Maria led by example and, in this way, inspired contemporary black feminists to reject roles secondary to men that were once prescribed for them as women behind the scenes (instead of on the front lines) of social protests. Moving from the private sphere to the public domain, black feminists today have come to resemble Maria more and more as they extend their influence beyond the home as wives and mothers to the world of work as public intellectuals, grassroots organizers, and career politicians. By so doing, they have adopted her distinct brand of activism. Intellectual activism, or "headwork" as Stewart called it, was democratizing and yielded radical analyses of injustice that emphasized self-help strategies, racial pride, and civil disobedience (Andrews 2003).

While no one can tell just how many people Stewart's writing and speeches have influenced, this chapter examines the determinants of black feminism—an intellectual tradition rooted in lived experience that made Stewart both a controversial writer and a salient figure during the nineteenth century. The tragic loss of her husband as well as the base tactics used by unscrupulous lawyers to rob Stewart of her rightful inheritance jump-started her distinguished career as a writer, educator, and lecturer. Recognizing these circumstances as determinate factors in the life of Stewart is essential to understanding the ways in which various forces and events shape the lives of individual black women as they similarly move through the world and face interlocking systems of oppression. The example of Stewart suggests that hardship and suffering can trigger black feminist activism and subsequently lead to the formation of black women's clubs, charitable organizations, and political alliances that benefit the larger community of black writers, educators, and lecturers. In the face of adversity, Stewart exhibited much poise and resiliency as she pursued positions of leadership and authority outside the domestic sphere and into the political realm. Religion was a major force in her life and, coincidently, it went hand in hand with her political agenda. Stewart practiced and preached an activist, woman-centered faith, whereby her religious convictions translated into formidable acts of resistance that blurred the boundaries between spiritual and secular affairs. While she weathered the storms that resulted from her efforts to speak on behalf of black civil rights and women's liberation, it was not without injury to her person when she constantly had to balance a variety of independent variables that made the pursuit for social justice ever so troublesome.

In light of Stewart's lived experience and the factors that seemingly explain her distinct brand of activism, this chapter offers a detailed discussion of several hypotheses that explain feminist consciousness in general and black feminist consciousness in particular. Using data from the 1993–1994 NBPS, I examine the impact of such factors as marital status, age, income, education, employment status, religiosity, place of residence, interviewer sex, race identification, and power discontent on black feminist consciousness, focusing on both the similarities and the differences in predictors for black male and female attitudes. This chapter then fills a void in the literature, augmenting our knowledge of black attitudes toward gender equality and feminist priorities, relative to Maria W. Stewart's own conversion process as she was widowed, robbed of her rightful inheritance, religiously inspired, and discontent with her lot in life.

Significance of Research

Much of the important work on the determinants of feminist consciousness focuses on the attitudes of white women but not black women. Almost completely absent is information on the determinants of black feminist consciousness for the adult African American population. Despite a number of scales that measure white attitudes toward gender equality and feminist priorities, few have captured black feminist voices or relied on black respondents for the development of such scales using a national survey. Existing scales often prevent the development of alternative scales comprised of differential measures that distinguish black women from other race-sex groups. If survey researchers and public opinion scholars could measure different feminist perspectives, they might then determine whether lived experiences with interlocking systems of oppression cause a shift in perspectives or some sort of "conversion" as reported by Maria W. Stewart that prompts active participation in public life. Another use of such a measure would be to determine the strength of distinct feminist perspectives within specific communities, or the same community over time, or after extraordinary events (e.g., the Clarence Thomas/Anita Hill controversy).

If public opinion scholars are interested in how individuals come to adopt feminist views, they must begin to consider whether variables that influence one feminist perspective have a similar effect on another. Much of the extant literature, however, is based on the American National Election Studies—data with too few African Americans to make reasonable comparisons between and among various race-sex groups (Henley et al. 1998). Prior research suggests that women are more likely to endorse feminist goals, support the women's liberation movement, and show high levels of feminist consciousness if they are highly educated, less religious, and employed in the paid labor force (Fulenwider 1980; Klein 1984; Anderson and Cook 1985). Other scholars have since examined attitudes within several nations, focusing on social structure and culture in an effort to extend the study of feminist politics beyond the United States (Davis and Robinson 1991; Wilcox 1991; Wilcox and Thomas 1992; Banaszak and Plutzer 1993a, 1993b; Togeby 1995). In most cases, these same scholars have focused either exclusively or primarily on structural or demographic determinants of feminist consciousness—not black feminist consciousness.

Given that few studies have explored the determinants of black feminist consciousness among African American women, and even fewer have explored the determinants of black feminist consciousness among African American women *and* men, this chapter investigates whether variables that predict attitudes toward feminism among white citizens have a similar effect on attitudes toward black feminism among African Americans and whether the determinants of black feminism differ for African American women and men when studied separately. By so doing, the chapter advances our knowledge of black feminism relative to prior research on white feminism and reveals the benefits of differentiating feminist perspectives. It is an in-depth discussion of various research hypotheses that explain feminist consciousness in general and black feminist consciousness in particular to which I now turn.

Education

According to a number of studies, education is one of the most important determinants of feminist support for men and women in general (Fulenwider 1980; Klein 1984; Cook 1989; Davis and Robinson 1991; Wilcox 1990, 1997; Banaszak and Plutzer 1993a, 1993b). Scholars suggest that individuals who are highly educated will be more conscious of gender inequality than individuals who are not. The explanation is that education familiarizes individuals with experiences different from their own (including those of the opposite sex) and inculcates ideals of fairness and equality for all. In light of this, Klein (1984) argued that educated women were more likely to reject traditional constraints imposed on them regarding job choices, salary, and chances for promotion. They were also more likely than those of less education to attribute lack of advancement to external forces. Thus, highly educated individuals will be more likely than those with less education to support black feminist ideals.

Income

While few scholars consider family income alone as a determinant of gender-related attitudes, there is literature to guide my expectations about the effects of income on black feminist attitudes. Wilcox (1997) reports that education and income predict both race and gender consciousness among black women. Like education, family income creates opportunities and lifestyle changes that in turn promote support for gender equality and feminist priorities. Klein (1984) suggests that working women who take on higher status, nontraditionally female occupations are more likely to be feminist than those who are confined to the home or low wage jobs that even today remain traditionally female occupations. Thus, I expect that individuals with high incomes will be more likely than individuals with low incomes to endorse black feminist tenets regardless of sex.

Employment Status

Several scholars suggest that women's labor force participation influences support for feminism (Fulenwider 1980; Klein 1984, 1987; Banaszak and Plutzer 1993a, 1993b). Like education and income, labor force participation creates opportunities and lifestyle changes that in turn promote support for gender equality and feminist priorities. It is the case that women's labor force participation "increases women's economic resources, dispels myths about women's inability to participate, and increases their power in family life" therefore having a liberalizing effect on gender role attitudes within the public and private realms (Banaszak and Plutzer 1993a, 149). Moreover, women's labor force participation gives women direct experience with sex disparities in earnings, promotion, and work conditions (Klein 1984; Davis and Robinson 1991). Black feminist scholars in particular have argued that black women reach full actualization of black feminist consciousness via day-to-day encounters with race, class, and gender oppression, which lead them to reject the occupationally segregated labor market where there are male and female jobs and black and white jobs (Stone 1979; hooks 1984, 1989; D. King 1988; Guy-Sheftall 1995; Collins 2000). Thus, I expect that black women working (either full time or part time) will be more likely than those black women who are not working outside of the home to endorse black feminist tenets.

Age

Several authors have described feminists as young women who came of age when attitudes toward traditional sex roles were changing (Fulenwider 1980; Klein 1984; Cook 1989; Wilcox 1991, 1997). During the 1960s and early 1970s, civil rights leaders and feminist activists solicited support from African American women through mobilization efforts directed toward "consciousness raising" and collective action. In both instances, African American women were called on to form alliances and engage in the struggle for equal rights. Wilcox (1990, 1997) identifies young black women who are well educated as most supportive of feminist beliefs. Similarly, Fulenwider (1980) points to age as an individual-level factor having implications for feminist attitudes among men and women. She finds that rising age is associated with a decline in feminism. Moreover, the relationship between age and feminism is stronger for women than men. Thus, I expect younger black women to be most supportive of black feminism.

Urban Residence

Fulenwider (1980) indicates that urban residence is associated with a rise in feminism. Apparently, women living in urban areas are less enamored with the occupationally segregated labor market than those living in smaller cities or towns. Klein (1984) suggests that urban communities offer more possibilities for nontraditional lifestyles than smaller rural communities. This suggests that the community in which a person lives will influence the individual's attitudes. Thus, black women and men living in urban areas are expected to uphold black feminist tenets.

Power Discontent

Some scholars argue that black women readily recognize disadvantage and discrimination due to their unique disadvantaged status (M. King 1975; Wilcox 1990; hooks 1984, 1989; Collins 2000). Since slavery, the fate of African American women has been tied to the socioeconomic status of the race as a whole (A. Davis 1981; Orfield and Ashkinaze 1991; Gooding-Williams 1993; Wilson 1996). The evidence to support this claim is quite clear. And while both African American women and men lag behind other race-sex groups on measures of socioeconomic well-being, it is the case that African American men benefit from patriarchy and enjoy some sense of privilege on account of their sex—specifically, in terms of their salary and promotion. For this reason, African American women are expected to be quite distinct in their feminist outlooks from African American men. Thus, the relationship between black feminism and power discontent will be stronger for these women than their black male counterparts.

Marital Status

Black feminist theorists assert that that there are many differences, both historically and in contemporary times, between the ways in which black women and white women experience sexism in this country. First, stereotypes of black and white women differ appreciably in this country (hooks 1984; Roberts 1997; Collins 1996, 2000). Historically, African American women were not put on pedestals and characterized as virtuous, warm, compassionate, intelligent, attractive, passive, or weak women (Fordham 1993; Weitz and Gordon 1993). Such traits were assigned to white women who supposedly epitomized femininity or femaleness. Universalizing (or normalizing) white womanhood set white women up as the norm against which black women were found lacking and appeared to be deviant cases that contrasted sharply with white femininity. African American women were characterized as loud, aggressive, argumentative, stubborn, and bitchy (Fordham 1993; Jewell 1993; Weitz and Gordon 1993). Such traits became most visible in prevailing images of black womanhood—the mammy, jezebel, black matriarch, and welfare queen—as they appeared in mass media outlets and represented the antithesis of white womanhood (A. Davis 1981; D. White 1985; Collins 1990; Jewell 1993; Roberts 1997).

Both the mammy and jezebel owe their existence to the institution of slavery under which female slaves worked on plantations as domestics and field hands. The mammy image served as the basis for Aunt Jemima, an obese African American woman, of dark complexion, with large breasts and buttocks, who willingly and jovially served white households (D. White 1985; Jewell 1993; Bogle 1995; Roberts 1997). The jezebel image served as the basis for the tragic mulatto, a thin African American woman, of fair complexion, with a slender nose and long straight hair, who sexually seduced white men (White 1985; Jewell 1993; Bogle 1995; Roberts 1997). While mammy assuaged white guilt and symbolized black–white relations at their best, jezebel excused the rape of female slaves on the plantation and put white women on a pedestal as morally superior (A. Davis 1981; Jewell 1993; Bogle 1995).

Both the black matriarch and welfare queen owe their existence to social science research—most notably, the work of Daniel Patrick Moynihan (1965). The image of the black matriarch served as the basis for today's welfare queen. Portrayed as overbearing and emasculating, the black matriarch was held accountable for the "tangle of pathology" that marked a stark increase in the number of single-parent, black female-headed households (A. Davis 1981; Roberts 1997; Neubeck and Cazenave 2001). Similarly, the welfare queen was blamed for perpetuating welfare dependency, transmitting a pathological lifestyle to children, and demoralizing black men. Depicted as a lazy mother on welfare, she deliberately bred children at the expense of taxpayers to increase her monthly check (A. Davis 1981; Roberts 1997; Neubeck and Cazenave 2001).

While the black matriarch gained widespread notoriety and directed critical attention away from structural barriers to black progress, the welfare queen effectively cast blame on the victim and provided a rationale to control the fertility of black mothers receiving public assistance (Roberts 1997; Collins 2000). Both the black matriarch and the welfare queen are depicted as bad mothers and marriage partners. Such prevailing images of black womanhood are promoted for political ends; enjoying widespread societal support, many individuals come to view African American women with contempt. African American women are then blamed for the disruption of black family life—fewer marriages, higher divorce rates, more absentee fathers, increased single-hood, more children born out of wedlock, and living below the poverty line.

Today, African American women of all classes remain ever so cognizant of such prevailing images and subsequently develop a "unique angle of vision" rooted in their lived experience with interlocking systems of oppression regardless of marital status. That is to say, the consequences of prevailing images of black womanhood that promote negative stereotypes of African American women affect both the private and the public domains of their lives. These prevailing images influence interpersonal relationships, public policy debates, the enforcement of laws, and criminal sentencing in this country (Tonry 1995; Roberts 1997; Jordan 1997; Bowen and Bok 1998; Gilens 1999). It is in this regard that the debate surrounding the Supreme Court's decision to review the University of Michigan's case on affirmative action becomes illustrative.

Given that affirmative action has long been a fiercely contested policy measure designed to remedy past discrimination, the importance of this case could not be overestimated. The outcome affected several colleges and universities that considered race as one factor amid others like community service, extracurricular activities, letters of recommendation, personal essays, and standardized test scores in their admissions decisions. Despite the fact that the Court exercised judicial restraint and upheld past precedent, thereby allowing affirmative action to continue, one nagging problem remained: the persistent achievement gap between black and white students on standardized tests. It is an issue that fueled much of the debate surrounding affirmative action, which usually was framed by mainstream media outlets in the most pejorative terms

(McCombs 1989). Critics, for example, charged that hard quotas resulted in lower standards and reverse discrimination. Such a political message in combination with racial stereotypes promote inappropriate challenges to African American women in various social and professional settings—in the supermarket, on the street, and at executive board meetings. Inappropriate challenges include, but are not limited to, loud outbursts, the use of profanity, abrupt exits, suggestive comments, and insolent e-mail messages—all of which violate standard harassment policies when directed at an individual or group because of their race, ethnicity, ancestry, national origin, sex, sexual orientation, age, and physical or mental disabilities. Bringing these two forces together—racial stereotypes and affirmative action debates—can invoke strong reactions from people and lead them to view African American women with disdain, especially when considering that their low status in the social hierarchy can sometimes clash with the high status of their occupational profession. It is in this regard that the black female college professor and her experiences in the white classroom become illustrative as she contradicts prevailing images of black womanhood (see, for example, P. Williams 1991; Benjamin 1997; Gregory 1999; Vargas 2002).

A compelling body of literature suggests that privileged white students continue to harbor myths and stereotypes based almost solely on their impressions of the most disadvantaged segment of the black population (Bohmer and Briggs 1991; Weitz and Gordon 1993; TuSmith and Reddy 2002). Still, they hold on to these stereotypes and use them to rate the performance of African American women faculty who do not represent the white heterosexual male norm (Weitz and Gordon 1993; Moore 1996; Baker and Copp 1997; Vargas 1999; Turner 2002). This norm seems to be quite natural and, in fact, neutral to the privileged white student who will experience difficulty in recognizing African American women faculty as both competent and qualified instructors when this alternative authority figure does not meet gendered expectations and emulate racial stereotypes. Critical to understanding this phenomenon is grasping that white students do not always see whiteness and its privileges as they move through the world (Delgado and Stefancic 1997). Instead, they remain ever so conscious of gender roles and stereotypes as they enjoy widespread societal support.

Selecting such social or physical characteristics as age, race, and sex that are typically identifiable, students discriminate and manage information to evaluate faculty who contrast with the white heterosexual male norm. When developing impressions of African American women faculty, students draw on prevailing images of black womanhood to form their opinions (Benjamin 1997; Gregory 1999; Vargas 1999). At the same time, students look for certain details about the instructor to confirm their gendered expectations and racial stereotyping—postures, speech patterns, and bodily gestures. Students might even go so far as to interpret any available information as confirming their self-fulfilling prophecies (Vargas 1999). Depending on the context, individual characteristics can become more salient and elicit greater stereotyping (S. Taylor 1981). Composed of primarily white heterosexual male faculty, the traditionally white university makes the social and physical characteristics of African American women faculty particularly salient. It casts white men as models of professorial authority, which sets the norm against which African American women are measured and found lacking authority when they are unable or unwilling to assume identical speech or cultural conventions as white heterosexual males. Thus, students hold fast to their gendered expectations and racial stereotypes and continue to view African American women as possessing traits that differ from the white heterosexual male norm.

The bottom line is this: African American women faculty who contradict prevailing images of black womanhood are often subjected to the same characterization of African American women as loud, aggressive, argumentative, stubborn, and bitchy. Being able to demonstrate sensitivity, warmth, and compassion are gendered expectations that students hold for women versus men faculty. African American women faculty, being black and female, are often evaluated on the basis of their ability to meet both these gendered expectations and racial stereotypes (Moore 1996; Baker and Copp 1997). Prior research suggests that students expect women faculty and faculty of color to be easier, assuming they will not have to perform as well (Moore 1996; Baker and Copp 1997). Moreover, students regard young looking women faculty easier to push around, less experienced, and more willing to make exceptions to rules (Moore 1996). African American women faculty, particularly those who are young, are surely disadvantaged by such student expectations based on their sex, race, and age.

Second, the traditional housewife model of womanhood has never been applicable to most African American women. African American women are more likely to be heads of households and historically their labor participation has exceeded that of white women (D. King 1988; Guy-Sheftall 1995). Compulsory labor has typically overshadowed every other aspect of black female experiences, including her role as wife, mother, and homemaker (A. Davis 1981; Jewell 1993; Browne 1999). Her employment in the workforce also begets concrete experiences with constant overt as well as covert discrimination through daily interactions with employers and coworkers who hold the same gendered expectations and racial stereotypes as the students described above. Those experiences, both individual and institutional, provide black women with a "unique angle of vision on self, community, and society" that stimulates a set of political beliefs about the equality of the sexes regardless of marital status (Collins 1990, 25). While other scholars have found that marital status predicts feminist consciousness among white women, my expectation is that marital status will *not* be a significant predictor for black women because the way in which black women and white women experience sexism in this country differs appreciably.

Race Identification

With empirical evidence, scholars have shown that a commitment to feminist principles does not detract from a sense of solidarity based on race (Robinson 1987; Wilcox 1990, 1997; Gay and Tate 1998; Simien and Clawson 2004). Wilcox (1990, 1997) argued that race consciousness has the potential to facilitate the development of feminist consciousness because black women who identified strongly with their race were more likely to uphold feminist views. Similarly, Robinson (1987) empirically tested two competing hypotheses about the effects of multiple group identity on black consciousness. One hypothesis suggested that black women who identify with blacks and women will possess a weaker sense of race consciousness than black women who identify solely with blacks. The other suggested that black women who identify with blacks and women will possess a stronger sense of race consciousness than black women who identify solely with blacks. In her analysis, Robinson constructed an interaction term that was the product of women's common fate and black common fate to measure multiple group identity. Demonstrating that gender identification differentially influenced the underlying dimensions of race consciousness by having a positive effect on power discontent, system blame, and no effect on collective action, Robinson concluded that gender identification among black women does not detract from race consciousness. Contrary to those who maintain that an emphasis on gender divides the black community and undermines black male leadership, the work of Robinson and Wilcox refuted these claims with empirical evidence. Thus, my expectation is that those who identify strongly with their race will support black feminist tenets more than those who do not.

Religiosity

In Wilcox's work, religiosity (frequency of prayer, closeness to God, frequency of church attendance, and church involvement) did not have a significant impact on feminist support among black women. This is worth noting because Pauline Stone (1979) and Frederick Harris (1999) attribute low levels of feminist consciousness among black women to high levels of religiosity. Stone, who lamented the low levels of feminist consciousness among black women, argued that the black church has validated the patriarchal nature of male–female relationships through sermon and teaching of sexual inequality. Similarly, Harris contended that "black women's exclusion from clerical leadership and key decision-making processes in their congregations" legitimizes black male authority and reinforces gender role stereotypes of black women as "doers" and "carriers" in charge of the private sphere (155). Harris, who examined support for women's clerical and political leadership, found that church attendance and active membership affect black women's support for gender equality. Black women who are most active in their churches are least supportive of the idea that black women should share equally in the political leadership of the black community and the notion that black churches or places of worship should allow more women to become members of the clergy. Thus, my expectation is that black citizens who frequently attend church and consciously identify themselves as active church members will subscribe less than others to black feminist principles and ideals.

Sex of Interviewer

Few social scientists have considered sex-of-interviewer effects. In "Interviewer Gender and Gender Attitudes," Emily Kane and Laura Macaulay (1993) found that male respondents offered significantly different responses to male and female interviewers when asked about gender equality. For example, male respondents were more likely to indicate that men and women divide child care, women have too little societal influence, men have too much societal influence, and occupational inequality is the result of gender discrimination when interviewed by a woman as opposed to a man. Kane and Macaulay also found that female respondents offered significantly different responses to male and female interviewers when asked questions pertaining to collective action strategies. For example, female respondents were more likely to support collective action strategies by women as well as government efforts related to occupational equality and child care when interviewed by a woman as opposed to a man. Therefore, my expectation is that the sex of the interviewer will affect black feminist support among black men (Kane and Macaulay 1993). Because the 1993–1994 NBPS does not include items that tap collective action strategies, I will not be able to test whether black women are more likely to support collective action strategies as well as government efforts that advance a black feminist agenda when interviewed by a woman.

Data and Measures

Using data from the 1993–1994 NBPS, this project examines closely the determinants of black feminist consciousness by including each predictor in a regression model. With a special focus on the differences in predictors for black men and women, I examine the relationship between black feminist support and measures of marital status, age, income, education, employment, religiosity, urban residence, interviewer sex, race identification, and status discontent. The measurement items chosen for age, marital status, urban residence, race identification, religiosity, income, education, status discontent, sex of the interviewer, and employment status have been examined previously and typically set the standard. They are validated measures from the landmark NES and the NBES. Comprised of those questions that best measure the aforementioned variables, this project replicates operational definitions that appear in prior studies. The exact wording of these questions and response choices may be found in Appendix B.

Socioeconomic Variables

The following socioeconomic variables were included in the analysis: education, income, and employment status. Education was simply measured by the number of years completed and coded as such in accordance with a 0 to 1 scale with 1 indicating the highest level of education. Income was measured by the question, "Which of the following income groups includes your total family income in 1992 before taxes?"

Up to $10,000	$30,000–$40,000
$10,000–$15,000	$40,000–$50,000
$15,000–$20,000	$50,000–$75,000
$20,000–$25,000	$75,000 and over
$25,000–$30,000	

The coding was from 0 (up to $10,000) to 1 (more than $75,000). Finally, employment status was measured by the question, "In terms of your main activity are you working full time, working part time, temporarily laid off, unemployed, retired, homemaker, a student, or are you permanently disabled?" Respondents who responded working full time or part time were coded 1. All others were coded 0.

Demographic Variables

The following demographic variables were included in the analysis: age, marital status, and gender. Age was measured by the question, "What was your age at your last birthday?" This item was coded as an eight-category variable:

$0 = 0–19$	$.57 = 50–59$
$.14 = 20–29$	$.71 = 60–69$
$.29 = 30–39$	$.86 = 70–79$
$.43 = 40–49$	$1 = 80+$

Marital status was measured by the question, "Are you currently married, widowed, separated, divorced, have you never been married, or are you living with a significant other?" Respondents who responded married were coded 0, and all others were coded 1. With regard to sex, males were coded 0 and females were coded 1.

Other Standard Predictors

The following standard predictors were included in the analysis: urban residence, power discontent, race identification, religiosity, and interviewer sex. Urban residence was measured by the question, "Do you live in a rural or country area, a small town, a suburb of a city, or in a large city?" Respondents who indicated a large city were coded 1. Those who indicated a suburb were coded .75, those who responded a small city were coded .5, and those who responded small town were coded .25. Finally, respondents who indicated rural or country were coded 0. Power discontent, another variable, was measured by two questions asking to what extent respondents felt that the economic position of blacks is better, about the same, or worse than whites, and to what extent respondents felt blacks were getting along economically.

Race identification was measured by a question asking to what degree respondents felt that what happened to blacks generally in this country affected their lives. Those who responded affirmatively were asked "Will it affect you a lot, some, or not very much?" Respondents who indicated a lot were coded 1, and were considered as having high race identification. Those who said some, were coded .66, those who replied not very much were coded .33, and respondents who said no were coded 0, and were considered as having low race identification.

Religiosity was measured by two questions: "How often do you attend religious services? Would you say at least once a week, once or twice a month, once or twice a year, or never?" Respondents who indicated never were coded 1. Those who responded once or twice a year were coded .66, and those who responded once or twice a month were coded .33. Finally, respondents who indicated once a week were coded 0. "Aside from attending regular services, in the past twelve months have you been an active member of your church or place of worship? I mean, have you served on a committee, given time to a special project, or helped to organize a meeting?" Respondents who indicated yes were coded 0, and those who indicated no were coded 1. Lastly, interviewer sex was coded in the same way as sex: males were coded 0, and females were coded 1.

Dependent Variable

Attitudes toward black feminism were measured by the same scale used in chapter 3, summing the answers to six questions concerning gender equality and feminist priorities within the black community. All variables were coded along a 0 to 1 scale with 1 indicating greater support for black feminist consciousness. Respondents were asked whether the problems of racism, poverty, and sexual discrimination are linked and should be addressed by the black community (ADDRESS ALL DISCRIMINATION). Respondents were also asked if they thought black women should share equally in the political leadership of the black community (BLACK WOMEN LEADERSHIP) and whether they supported more women becoming members of the clergy in black churches (MORE WOMEN CLERGY). Black citizens were asked whether they thought black feminist groups help the black community by advancing the position of black women or divide the black community (FEMINISTS HELP COMMUNITY) and whether black women suffered from both sexism within the black movement and racism within the women's movement (BOTH MOVE-MENTS). Finally, respondents were asked whether they thought what happens generally to black women in this country had something to do what happens in their own life (LINKED FATE WITH BLACK WOMEN).

DV = Black Fem consciousness

Analysis and Results

I began by examining the relationship between the dependent variable (black feminist consciousness) and several independent variables. More specifically, multiple linear regression analysis was used to ascertain the effect of age, education, income, race identification, employment status, religiosity, interviewer sex, marital status, urban residence, and power discontent on black feminist consciousness, focusing on differences in the predictors for black male and female attitudes. In this analysis, I present the results separately for black women and men (see tables 4.1 and 4.2). I then test whether the differences are statistically significant by using interaction terms in a model including both black women and men.

In keeping with expectations stated earlier in this chapter, the relationship between younger age and rising feminism was significant for black women. This was not the case for black men. Higher education was also a strong predictor of black feminist consciousness, as was income for black women. This was not the case for black men. Higher education was not a significant predictor of black feminist consciousness for black men. However, income was indeed a strong predictor for black men.

There was little support for the hypothesis suggesting that black women working either full time or part time would be more likely to endorse black feminist tenets. In other words, the hypothesis was not confirmed because women's employment status had no significant effect on their support for black feminist ideals. This might be due to the fact that black women (working or not) reach full actualization of black feminist consciousness via day-to-day encounters with race, class, and gender oppression on the street, in the supermarket, and in other public spheres.

Table 4.1
Determinants of Black Feminist Consciousness,
Estimated Separately by Gender

Independent Variable	Black Women	Black Men
EDUCATION	.253**	.052
	(.078)	(.113)
INCOME	.107**	.160**
	(.038)	(.053)
EMPLOYMENT STATUS	−.037	.014
	(.020)	(.029)
AGE	−.152**	−.086
	(.036)	(.056)
URBAN RESIDENCE	.037	−.011
	(.027)	(.040)
POWER DISCONTENT	.090**	.043
	(.042)	(.056)
MARITAL STATUS	.003	.025
	(.020)	(.026)
RACE IDENTIFICATION	.163**	.207**
	(.023)	(.037)
RELIGIOSITY	.035	.049
	(.027)	(.037)
INTERVIEWER SEX	.023	.046*
	(.018)	(.025)
CONSTANT	.372**	.353**
	(.054)	(.080)
ADJUSTED R^2	.185	.196

Source: 1993 National Black Politics Study.

Table entries are ordinary least squares regression coefficients, followed by the associated standard error. *$p < .05$; **$p < .01$; for 2-tailed test.

Urban residence did not affect the level of support for black feminist consciousness for either sex. This was unexpected. It was predicted that urban residence would be a significant predictor of black feminism because urban communities offer more possibilities for nontraditional lifestyles than smaller rural communities (Klein 1984). It is probably the case that black women and men reach full actualization of black feminist consciousness via day-to-day encounters with race, class, and gender oppression in both rural and urban communities. Hence, urban residence would not explain the development of black feminist consciousness among black women and men as it does for white women in urban communities.

Power discontent was associated with black feminist support among black women. This was not the case for black men. As has already been suggested, black women and men share a common experience with race oppression and class exploitation. However, it is the case that black men benefit from patriarchy on account of their sex. For this reason, black women were expected to be quite distinct in their feminist outlooks from black men. Given that African American women occupy the lower stratum in the occupational structure in the United States, it is quite possible that they are cognizant of their unique disadvantaged status in comparison to white men, black men, and white women.

It was predicted that marital status would not be a significant predictor of black feminist support among black women because the stereotypical roles of white women and black women in this country differ appreciably (M. King 1975; A. Davis 1981; Jewell 1993). This prediction was confirmed. Considering that previous research has consistently found that marital status is a key factor in determining white women's support for feminist principles, this finding is certainly worth noting because it bolsters my claim that there is a clear difference between black and white women in their relationship to feminism.

Consistent with my expectations, race identification was a significant predictor of black feminist support for both sexes. Those black women and men who identified strongly with their race were most supportive of black feminist consciousness. Given the long-standing debate in the black community that black feminist consciousness detracts from race consciousness, the fact that both black women and men who identify strongly with their race are more likely to support feminist tenets is significant.

Religiosity did not predict black feminist support for black women or men. This is indeed meaningful. Scholars have debated whether the black church inhibits the development of feminist consciousness via sermons and teaching about the patriarchal nature of male–female relationships or promotes the development of feminist consciousness via sermons and teaching about civil rights and black liberation. This finding in particular suggests that frequency of church attendance and active church membership neither impedes nor encourages the development of black feminist consciousness as it has been defined and measured here.

Sex of the interviewer has a significant, although small, impact on support for black feminism among black men. Men demonstrated higher levels of black feminist consciousness when interviewed by a woman. This was not the case for black women; interviewer sex did not impact the level of support for black feminism among black women. While this finding suggests deference on the part of black men, it also indicates the importance of studying sex-of-interviewer effects in survey research. Given that research on sex-of-interviewer effects is notably rare, I hope that future research will test this possibility in more detail.

Obviously, there are important differences between black women and men in their relationship to feminism. For black women, strong predictors are education, income, age, race identification, and power discontent. Race identification and education are the strongest predictors, followed by age. Apparently, black women who are better educated with higher incomes are more likely to support black feminism. These women are also younger, highly race conscious, and most discontented with their lot in life. Together, these variables explain 18.5 percent of the variance in black feminist consciousness among black women. For black men, strong predictors are income, race identification, and interviewer sex. Race identification and income are the strongest predictors, followed by interviewer sex. Apparently, these men who possess higher incomes and identify strongly with their race are more likely to support black feminist tenets. At the same time, interviewer sex matters. These men are more likely to give the black feminist response when interviewed by a woman. Together, these variables explained approximately 19.6 percent of the variance in black feminist consciousness among black men. Both race identification and income are predictive variables for African American women and men alike, explaining their support for black feminism. More specifically, those African Americans with higher incomes are likely to possess both race consciousness and black feminist consciousness. It goes to show that race, gender, and class identities are interlocking and cannot be easily separated from the equation.

In the final analysis, black men and women were studied together. Results appear in table 4.2, which includes gender as a main effect and numerous interaction terms. Strong predictors of

Table 4.2
Overall Determinants of Black Feminist Consciousness

Independent Variable	Both Sexes
EDUCATION	.054
	(.113)
INCOME	.150**
	(.052)
EMPLOYMENT STATUS	.013
	(.029)
AGE	−.091
	(.055)
URBAN RESIDENCE	.022
	(.022)
POWER DISCONTENT	.037
	(.056)
MARITAL STATUS	.011
	(.016)
RACE IDENTIFICATION	.209**
	(.036)
RELIGIOSITY	.049
	(.037)
INTERVIEWER SEX	.047 *
	(.024)
GENDER	.027
	(.089)
GENDER X EDUCATION	.199
	(.138)
GENDER X INCOME	−.037
	(.062)
GENDER X AGE	−.056
	(.065)
GENDER X POWER DISCONTENT	.055
	(.070)
GENDER X RACE IDENTIFICATION	−.045
	(.043)
GENDER X INTERVIEWER SEX	−.023
	(.030)
GENDER X RELIGIOSITY	−.012
	(.046)
GENDER X EMPLOYMENT STATUS	−.051
	(.035)
CONSTANT	.343
	(.075)
ADJUSTED R^2	.196

Source: 1993 National Black Politics Study.

Table entries are unstandardized ordinary least squares regression coefficients, followed by the associated standard error. *p $\leq$ .05; **p $\leq$ .01; for 2-tailed test.

black feminist consciousness were income, interviewer sex, and race identification. Together, these variables explained approximately 19.6 percent of the variance in black feminist consciousness for both sexes. Interaction terms were added to the regression model for the purpose of examining whether the differences in such predictors as education, interviewer sex, age, and power discontent were statistically significant. Not one interaction term was statistically significant. This suggests that the differences in such predictors as education, interviewer sex, age, and power discontent for both sexes when studied apart are not significant. Thus, I conclude that both African American men and women have come to develop a shared understanding of their unique disadvantaged status amid such discriminatory practices as steering and blockbusting by realtors, redlining by banks and loan companies, de facto segregating of schools, and racial profiling by law enforcement that persists today. Ever so cognizant of past discrimination—slave codes, de jure segregation, literacy tests, white primaries, grandfather clauses, and lynching—contemporary examples of racial discrimination only serve to reinforce knowledge processes rooted in experience that remind individual members of the race of the stigma attached to them and the disadvantages derived from their inferior position vis-à-vis whites in the social, economic, and political structure of the United States.

Conclusion

Starting with the life history of Maria W. Stewart, this chapter drew critical attention to the religious conversion that immediately followed the death of her husband, James W. Stewart. Perhaps the most tragic event in her life, this terrible loss, in addition to the base tactics used by unscrupulous lawyers to rob Maria of her inheritance, surely inspired her call for racial solidarity, self-help, and civil disobedience before an assembly of her peers. A reasonable response to her personal misfortune, Maria's distinct brand of intellectual activism enabled others to think critically about the interrelationship between spiritual faith and political activism. To her, the relationship between the two was a reciprocal one of which public service was an inevitable outcome. Maria demonstrated that women of any race could speak ever so eloquently with moral authority on black civil rights and women's liberation during a period when such a public act of defiance was highly controversial. Similarly, the present chapter dares to reclaim an intellectual tradition that is distinctly black and feminist when the ideas and experiences of African American women have been largely ignored and marginalized in political science. By focusing on such predictive factors as marital status, age, income, education, employment status, religiosity, place of residence, interviewer sex, race identification, and power discontent, I recognize the importance of everyday living and those factors that shape black feminist perspectives for African American men and women alike.

While several studies have focused almost entirely on white women either per se or in comparison to white men, this study constitutes the first to examine fully the determinants of black feminist consciousness using a national survey of the adult African American population. Given the absence of literature on the determinants of black feminist consciousness, the focus of this analysis is long overdue. Using data from the 1993–1994 NBPS, I have found that education, income, power discontent, race identification, and age predict African American women's support for black feminist ideals. Neither urban residence nor marital status accounts for black feminist support among African American women and men. Moreover, employment status and religiosity do not explain support for black feminism within either sex. I have also found that income, race identification, and interviewer sex determine African American men's support for black feminist tenets. Common to both sexes were the variables race identification and income. Interaction terms were added to the regression model for the purpose of examining whether the differences in the two models, whereby black women and men were studied separately, were statistically significant when both sexes were studied together. Not one interaction term was statistically significant, which means that the differences in such predictors as education, interviewer sex, age, and power discontent were not consequential. Having developed a distinct perspective rooted in their shared experiences with interlocking systems of oppression, African American women and men are more similar than different in the causes of their beliefs toward gender equality and feminist priorities due to their social location in the United States.

Arguably, individual (or ascriptive) characteristics are less important than those factors rooted in lived experience that make one ever so aware of the persistence of structural inequality. Assuming that one must be both black and female to possess black feminist consciousness is problematic, especially when considering that African American women share common experiences with other race-sex groups that speak to the unequal distribution of costs and benefits, as well as structural and institutional arrangements that facilitate intergroup cooperation and multigroup gain. That is not to say absolute agreement exists between and among individual members of various race-sex groups when ideological and intellectual commitments are not biologically determined by chromosomal, hormonal, or other physiological traits. But objective conditions and concrete experiences warrant the development of black feminist consciousness—the ability to recognize that African American women face discrimination on the basis of race and gender—among various race-sex groups. African American women are not the only group who struggle with multiple identities and, for this reason, it is quite possible for other race-sex groups to be cognizant of and sympathetic toward the particular predicament of black women because they too suffer from race oppression, class exploitation, gender discrimination, and heterosexism in contemporary American society.

African Americans in general and African American women in particular are positioned differently from other people in the United States and their distinct brand of political activism arises from day-to-day experiences with meanings, practices, and structural conditions that limit their lives as they are located at the bottom of the social, economic, and political hierarchy. Structural inequality then influences the wants, interests, and desires of African American men and women as they are expressed both verbally and nonverbally in public and private domains. Given the unequal distribution of power and privilege in the United States, they develop similar kinds of knowledge about the workings of society and have similar kinds of routine experiences in which they respond to individually or collectively. Overcoming interlocking systems of oppression has inspired African American men and women to participate actively in individual and collective forms of resistance—slave revolts, migrations, economic boycotts, sit-ins, freedom rides, court cases, nonviolent demonstrations, campaigns, and elections—all in an effort to secure basic citizenship rights and influence the American political system.

Having moved from protests to politics in this post–civil rights era, African Americans have since become more active in the policymaking process, specializing in research, coalition building, and constituency development. The black politics agenda has expanded to include affirmative action, unemployment, environmental racism, welfare reform, teenage pregnancy, drug abuse, criminal sentencing, and AIDS, among other issues. That is not to say that individual members of the race will respond uniformly and create specific outcomes that advance the black liberation struggle when some black people will accept and others will reject the significance of race and the necessity of direct action. While black intellectuals are often criticized for ideological posturing and race rhetoric, radical actors are praised for their efforts to mobilize the masses and arrange organized protests. Interrogating how well or poorly black intellectuals serve the masses for which they speak and write about has become the pastime of those working at the grassroots level alongside the most vulnerable to oppression. Few black intellectuals leave the classroom and lecture hall to pursue revolutionary causes that involve nonelite actors and thinkers outside of academe. Rather than earn the trust of nonelite civil servants through critical action and collective struggle, black intellectuals typically operate in isolation and confine themselves to the Ivory Tower, espousing sophisticated critiques of all that ails the larger black community (for which they usually possess no direct contact) within peer reviewed journals and scholarly books for the sole purpose of tenure and promotion.

Robert C. Smith's *We Have No Leaders: African Americans in the Post–Civil Rights Era* (1996) is one such example that provides a scathingly provocative account of the effects and importance of the past three decades on the future of black politics. Using archival and interview data, Smith argues that black leadership has been ineffective in maintaining viable and effective organizations post–civil rights. Out of this analysis of continuity and innovation in black organizations emerges the claim that while black leaders have somewhat adapted to post–civil rights era circumstances, some serious problems still impede effective black political participation (McClain 1996; Smith 1996). While sophisticated critiques are certainly useful and expose errors of the past, they are not surrogates for direct action or social justice campaigns that subvert oppressive conditions and build formidable alliances. Like Maria W. Stewart, black intellectuals must act as agents of change and make something of unjust power relations that affirm their existence and relevance to the larger black community. Using their knowledge of the shortcomings inherent to black organizations, activist scholars reject a top-down hierarchical model of organization and strategy that emphasizes elite interaction versus constituent mobilization. In pursuit of higher moral and political objectives outside of academe, they exhibit the capacity for networking within and between marginalized groups by tapping indigenous resources, mobilizing the vote as an independent force, and adhering to the norms of inclusive communicative democracy so as to attend to the specific needs of disadvantaged groups (James 1997; Young 2000; Ransby 2003). By so doing, activist scholars earn trust and renew faith in elite actors due to their involvement at the grassroots level in close proximity to nonelite actors and civil rights struggle. The point is: consciousness must translate to political behavior, as in the case of Maria W. Stewart, who exhibited a distinct brand of intellectual and political activism.

Chapter Five

BLACK FEMINIST CONSCIOUSNESS, RACE CONSCIOUSNESS, AND BLACK POLITICAL BEHAVIOR

A white woman has only one handicap to overcome—a great one, true, her sex. A colored woman faces two—her sex and her race. A colored man has only one—that of race.

—Mary Church Terrell,
A Colored Woman in a White World

In 1863, Mary Church Terrell was born in Memphis, Tennessee. Both of her parents were former slaves; however, neither one experienced the hardships of plantation life (Sterling 1979). Her father, Robert Church, was considered the richest black man in Memphis and perhaps the first black millionaire in the South. He secured his wealth at a time when the yellow fever epidemic plagued the residents of Memphis and many of them abandoned their homes. Robert Church purchased much of the property they left behind and pursued several business ventures, including a beauty parlor, a barbershop, and a saloon (B. Jones 1990). Mary's mother, Louisa, owned and operated a hair salon where only the wealthiest women had their beauty needs met. Despite her parents' wealth, however, Mary did not live in isolation from the world and experienced racial prejudice at an early age.

While on a trip with her father aboard a railroad train, she was humiliated by the conductor. Before retiring to the smoker for a cigar, Robert Church seated his five-year-old daughter in the first-class coach. Mary, who was neatly dressed and on her best behavior, was startled when the conductor asked, "Whose little nigger is this?" and insisted that she be seated in the Jim Crow car. Frightened, Mary stood in the aisle (Sterling 1979, 123). Her father, who was fair enough to pass for white, ordered that the conductor leave his child alone. The man reluctantly obeyed this command, but continued to glare at the little girl for the remainder of the trip. This event and the experiences that followed it made Mary ever so aware of black–white relations. Thus, to fully appreciate the historic significance of Mary Church Terrell, it is necessary to understand the degree to which her consciousness emerged out of and transformed everyday life experiences with interlocking systems of oppression into formidable acts of resistance.

Rather than attend the segregated schools in Memphis, Mary's parents sent her to an integrated "model school" on the campus of Antioch College in Yellow Springs, Ohio. Once she got older, she attended Oberlin College where she received a bachelor of arts degree in 1884. After graduation she taught the basics of reading and writing at Wilberforce University in Ohio—the first American institution of higher learning for blacks—and later, she moved to Washington, D.C., to teach Latin at the Preparatory School for Colored Youth. While teaching at the Colored High School, Mary completed requirements for the master of arts degree for Oberlin College in 1888. She then traveled to Europe where she spent two years learning French, German, and Italian. By 1891, Mary had returned to the United States and married Robert Terrell—the first black person to graduate from Harvard University.

Certainly one of the most articulate and best educated black women in the late nineteenth century, Mary Church Terrell rejected traditional roles for women. She abandoned the purely domestic sphere and exhibited a great deal of independence through her travels abroad, educational experiences, and issue advocacy networks. Determined to make her life both useful and meaningful, Terrell became a prominent figure central in the women's club movement and its leading organization the National Association of Colored Women (NACW).

One of the founders and the first president of the NACW, Terrell made the elevation of the race her primary goal. While the NACW aided primarily black women and children, Terrell maintained that the organization reached the "source of many race problems" by supporting black family life (Jones 1990, 24). Kindergartens and day-care nurseries were established to provide much needed services to working mothers. Both "Mothers' Clubs" and "Homes for Girls" were created to dispense knowledge about the best methods for child rearing, conducting homes, and improving moral standards. They offered classes in domestic arts and served as employment bureaus for girls who found themselves excluded from the YMCA and similar white organizations (hooks 1981; Jones 1990; D. White 1999). By 1901, the NACW had become one of the most viable women's associations in the United States. The programs and objectives of the organization were advertised in a monthly newsletter, *The National Notes*. Conventions were held in major cities with large black populations—Nashville, Tennessee (1897), Chicago, Illinois (1899), and Buffalo, New York (1901). As a result, membership increased significantly.

By the turn of the century, Mary Church Terrell had firmly established herself as a spokeswoman for women's suffrage and black civil rights. A charter member of the NAACP, she became a popular lecturer and wrote many articles that appeared in magazines and newspapers across the country. She fought tirelessly to ensure civil rights compliance, equitable treatment under the law, desegregated lunch counters, and the right to vote for women. She actively participated in politics by various means: class action lawsuits, protest marches, economic boycotts, lunch counter sit-ins, local campaigns, and presidential elections. She lobbied Congress and state legislatures for antilynching legislation and ratification of the Nineteenth Amendment (hooks 1981). Such political activities carved out a special place for Mary Church Terrell as one of the most influential race leaders of her time.

In light of Terrell's accomplishments and the factors that seem to explain her distinct brand of activism, this chapter develops and tests a theory of the effect of two models—socioeconomic status and group consciousness—on black political behavior. Resource-based models of political participation suggest that African American women's increasing education, work experience, and organizational involvement boost the likelihood of political activity (Baxter and Lansing 1981; Ransford and Miller 1983; Dugger 1988; Barret 1995, 1997; Cohen, Jones, and Tronto 1997; Lein 1998). One might think of it this way: Terrell's access to education, wealth, and prestigious occupations explains her sense of civic duty and engagement in various modes of political behavior—signing petitions, contacting public officials, attending protest rallies, participating in marches, donating money, and sponsoring fund-raisers. That is to say, active participation in politics is a function of individual resources—socioeconomic status and group consciousness. African American women, like Mary Church Terrell, have long been active in ways not always tapped by conventional research on political behavior: grassroots activism, consciousness-raising efforts, issue advocacy networks, and volunteer service. Nonetheless, few scholars have demonstrated the critical importance of race consciousness as a determinant of political activism. Even fewer scholars have investigated the simultaneous effects of race and gender consciousness on black political behavior. All things considered, the example of Mary Church Terrell as she had access to resources that allowed her to defy gendered norms and pursue activist goals underscores the importance of considering whether black feminist consciousness in addition to race consciousness serves as an impetus for active participation in politics.

The empirical analyses that follow provide the first material link between those scholars who have written on black feminism and those who have focused on black political participation. Here, I empirically test various research hypotheses about the overall impact of specific strands of group consciousness on various modes of black political participation. The standard socioeconomic model used most often to predict black political participation is expanded to include *both* race consciousness *and* black feminist consciousness. By so doing, the present study contributes to our practical and theoretical understanding of black political participation.

Socioeconomic Status

The standard socioeconomic model of black political participation typically incorporates a lengthy list of predictors and assumes that socioeconomic resources predispose individuals to psychological orientations that spur political activity. The scholarship supporting this statement has remained fairly consistent (Olsen 1970; Verba and Nie 1972; Wolfinger and Rosenstone 1980; Leighley 1990,

1995; Conway 1991; Tate 1994; Dawson 1994). Educational institutions equip voters with participatory resources, including social and political contacts, economic opportunities, and access to government. Upper-class individuals are more likely than lower-class citizens to actively participate in politics because upper-class citizens feel as though they can be effective in both nonpolitical and political matters. In other words, upper-class citizens participate because they realize that they possess the skills and motivation to be successful. Empirical evidence further supports these claims by demonstrating that individuals with high levels of education and high incomes are more likely to participate in politics than individuals with low levels of education and low incomes (Angus et al. 1960; Verba and Nie 1972; Wolfinger and Rosenstone 1980; Conway 1991; Rosenstone and Hansen 1993). The effect of income on political participation is typically less than that of education. Thus, I hypothesize that black citizens who possess higher levels of education and income will be more likely to participate.

Group Consciousness

Miller et al. (1981) were among the first to explain mass political behavior for black citizens, women, and the poor (Leighley and Vedlitz 1999). Research in political science, psychology, and sociology has suggested that members of disadvantaged groups, particularly black citizens, participate at higher rates than whites because race consciousness spurs group cohesion and political mobilization (e.g., Olsen 1970; Verba and Nie 1972; Shingles 1981; Leighley and Vedlitz 1999). Unfortunately, few studies consider the full complexity of race consciousness and gender consciousness.

Race consciousness is a complex concept that includes four components: race identification, power discontent, system blame, and collective action orientation (Miller et al. 1981; Gurin 1985; Gurin, Hatchett, and Jackson 1989) The first component, race identification, involves a "perceived self-location" within a particular racial group and a sense of belonging or closeness to that group (Miller et al. 1981, 495). The second component, power discontent, reflects recognition of and disenchantment with the status deprivation of one's racial group. The third component, system blame, is an awareness that structural barriers rather than personal failings account for the subordinate status of the race. The fourth component, collectivist action orientation, represents a commitment to group strategies in confronting racism. Similarly, gender consciousness is a complex concept whereby the same four components are applied to the group consciousness of women (Gurin 1985).

However, black feminist consciousness is empirically distinct from race consciousness and gender consciousness. Black feminist consciousness is a complex concept that includes several interrelated attitudes and beliefs derived from the ideas and experiences of black women. It is defined by several underlying themes that delineate the contours of black feminist thought: intersectionality, gender equality, black feminism benefits the black community, and linked fate with black women. The first, intersectionality, involves an acute sense of awareness that the struggle to eradicate racism and sexism is rooted in yet another "ism" that plagues humanity: classism. The second is the acceptance of the belief that gender inequality exists within the context of the black community, and the third is the acceptance of the belief that feminism benefits the black community by advancing the agenda of black women. Finally, linked fate involves an acute sense of belonging or conscious loyalty to the group in question (i.e., black women) because of shared experience. In this instance, the individual who identifies with the group label has come to realize that individual life chances are inextricably tied to the group.

Other Standard Predictors

Several scholars have argued that other variables are important controls in behavioral models of political participation (Wolfinger and Rosenstone 1980; Rosentone and Hansen 1993; Verba, Schlozman et al. 1995; Timpone 1998). It is the case that church attendance reflects an individual's integration into the social milieu and research has shown that those individuals who frequently attend church participate at higher rates (Calhoun-Brown 1999; Harris 1999). Like church attendance, marital status reflects an individual's integration into the social milieu and previous studies have found this individual attribute to be related to electoral participation (e.g., Timpone 1998). Previous research has also reported gender disparities in political participation indicating that men are more likely than women to participate in various kinds of activities, most notably contributing money and working for a campaign (Rosenstone and Hansen 1993; Verba, Burns, and Schlozman 1997). Other variables added to the regression model include urban residence, age, and home ownership. These factors are likely to explain why some individuals engage in politics and others do not.

Hypotheses

The specific hypotheses that I test are:

H1: Black citizens who possess higher levels of education will be more likely to participate than those who do not.

H2: Black citizens who possess higher levels of income will be more likely to participate than those who do not.

H3: Black citizens who possess race consciousness will participate at higher levels than those who do not.

H4: Black citizens who possess black feminist consciousness will participate at higher levels than those who do not.

H5: Black citizens who frequently attend church will participate at higher levels than those who do not.

H6: Black citizens who are married will participate at higher levels than those who are not.

H7: Black men will be more likely to participate than black women in various kinds of political activities.

Data, Operational Definitions, and Measures

Since the purpose of this study is to examine the effect of two models—socioeconomic status and group consciousness—on black political behavior, the most useful data set on which to rely is the 1993–1994 NBPS. It is a unique study in that it contains questions that measure both race consciousness and black feminist consciousness. There are also several distinct forms of participation that can be examined using the 1993–1994 NBPS.

Political Participation

In this analysis, political participation is taken to mean those efforts by citizens to influence the selection of elected officials, or public policy outputs (Verba and Nie 1972; Guterbock and London 1983; Beckwith 1986; Conway 1991; Rosenstone and Hansen 1993; Verba, Schlozman et al. 1995). It is important to note that there are several types or modes of political participation. Voting is merely one type. Here, I consider an array of political activities that require varying degrees of initiative on the part of the citizen. Political scientists suggest that each type can be distinguished in terms of difficulty or desired impact on government. It is the case that some activities require more initiative than others and black citizens will engage in activities requiring the least amount of motivation. This is due to the lack of resources—money, civic skills, and time—that have been shown to influence the likelihood of political participation (Angus et al. 1960; Verba and Nie 1972; Rosenstone and Hansen 1993; Verba, Schlozman et al. 1995; Timpone 1998). Thus, citizens who participate in electoral and governmental politics tend to come from the most advantaged sectors of society. Typically, they are wealthy, well-educated Americans. They also tend to be more informed, politically interested, and efficacious than others (Rosenstone and Hansen 1993).

Of all types of political participation, presidential election turnout is thought to be the easiest because political parties, media outlets, and campaign organizations try hardest to mobilize the electorate during national elections (Verba and Nie 1972; Wolfinger and Rosenstone 1980; Beckwith 1986). The basic argument is that voting does not require as much attention to politics or as much knowledge about politics (Angus et al. 1960; Verba and Nie 1972; Rosenstone and Hansen 1993; Verba, Schlozman et al. 1995). Signing a petition constitutes another political activity that is among the least difficult to engage in because it requires little personal initiative on the part of the citizen (Verba and Nie 1972;

Rosenstone and Hansen 1993). Both the act of voting and signing a petition yield collective outcomes through cooperative behavior among citizens (Verba and Nie 1972; Rosenstone and Hansen 1993; Verba, Schlozman et al. 1995). It is argued here that voting, signing a petition in support of a specific candidate, and signing a petition in support of or against something are indirect forms of communicating messages to government officials (Verba and Nie 1972; Verba, Schlozman et al. 1995). Direct contact behavior, on the other hand, constitutes a more difficult political activity to engage in because it requires much initiative on the part of the citizen. As Verba and Nie (1972) have suggested, citizens decide whom to contact, when to contact the person, and why to do so. Communal and campaign activities are also among the most difficult participatory acts to engage in because such political engagement involves volunteerism on the part of the citizen—hours devoted to the campaign, dollars contributed to the candidate, communications dispatched to various media outlets, and protests attended (Verba and Nie 1972; Guterbock and London 1983; Beckwith 1986; Rosenstone and Hansen 1993; Verba, Schlozman et al. 1995).

Given that political acts vary in the extent to which they influence public policy and engage the general public, the various forms of political participation cited above are factor analyzed to determine dimensionality. Having undergone several stages of factor analysis, weakly correlated or ambiguous survey items will be discarded. The resulting factor will be comprised of those questions that best measure political participation. The measurement items chosen for political participation have been examined previously. They are validated measures from the landmark National Election Studies and the National Black Election Studies. Comprised of those questions that best measure political participation, this project replicates operational definitions that typically set the standard. For example, respondents were asked whether they had voted in the last presidential election, contacted a public official, attended a protest rally, signed a petition, helped in a voter registration drive, donated money to a political candidate, or handed out campaign material. The exact wording of these questions may be found in the codebook for the 1993–1994 NBPS. See Appendix D for complete question wording, response choices, and coding of variables.

Race Consciousness

The 1993–1994 NBPS contained questions measuring the four components of race consciousness: race identity, system blame, power discontent, and collective action orientation. Race identification was determined by respondents' feelings of linked fate with blacks (LINKED FATE WITH BLACKS). To measure system blame, I used four items that focused on how fair respondents considered the American legal system and society in general (UNFAIR OPPORTUNITY, UNFAIR DEAL, SOCIETY UNFAIR, UNFAIR LEGAL SYSTEM). Power discontent was assessed based on respondents' evaluations of the economic position of blacks as a group (BLACK ECONOMICS) and black citizens in comparison to white citizens (BLACK VS. WHITE ECONOMICS). Typically, scholars use items that measure discontent with political power, rather than economic power (Gurin 1985; Gurin, Hatchett, and Jackson 1989; Miller et al. 1981). Economic discontent items were used as surrogates for political discontent. Given the overlap between political and economic power in the United States, prior researchers have accepted economic discontent items as acceptable substitutes for political discontent. Two items measured collective action. One item asked to what degree black citizens felt that the movement for black rights had affected them personally (BLACK MOVEMENT). Another item asked whether the respondent was a member of any organization working to improve the status of black people in this country (BLACK ORGANIZATION). See Appendix C for complete question wording and response choices.

A superior measure of race consciousness could have incorporated the separate indicators for system blame, power discontent, and collective action orientation available in the 1984–1988, and 1996 NBES. One item asked whether racial discrimination was still a problem (SYSTEM BLAME). Another item asked whether black people should organize collectively to have power and improve their position in the United States (COLLECTIVE ACTION ORIENTATION). Other items asked whether [whites, blacks] have too much influence, just about the right amount of influence, or too little influence (POWER DISCONTENT).

Black Feminist Consciousness

Given that there is not one single item that captures every aspect of black feminist consciousness, the concept is measured by a total of six items. Of these items, one asks, "Do you think what happens generally to black women in this country will have something to do with what happens in your life?" Respondents who answer affirmatively are then asked "Will it affect you a lot, some, or not very much?" This item (LINKED FATE WITH BLACK WOMEN) measures the degree to ⟨...⟩ erceive that their fate is linked to t⟨...⟩ asis of their shared experience in thi⟨...⟩ respondents whether the problems ⟨...⟩ discrimination are all linked toge⟨...⟩ ssed by the black community (ADD⟨...⟩N). Respondents were also asked w⟨...⟩ men should share equally in the po⟨...⟩ community (BLACK WOMEN LEADERSHIP) and whether they supported more women becoming members of the clergy in black churches (MORE WOMEN CLERGY). Black citizens were asked whether they thought black feminist groups helped the black community by advancing the position of black women or divide the black community (FEMINIST HELP COMMUNITY) and whether black women suffered from both sexism within the black movement and racism within the women's movement (BOTH MOVEMENTS).

A superior measure of black feminist consciousness could have incorporated the separate indicators for system blame, collective action orientation, and power discontent used by Wilcox (1997) from the 1984 NBES. One item asks whether sex discrimination is a real problem for black and white women in this country (SYSTEM BLAME). Another item asks whether the best way for black women to handle problems of sex discrimination is to work together as a group (COLLECTIVE ACTION ORIENTATION). Another item asks whether black women should organize among themselves only or work together with all women (COLLECTIVE ACTION ORIENTATION). Unfortunately, these items were only asked of women. Thus, the political attitudes and political behavior of these women could not be compared to those of men. Other items asked whether [men, women] possess too much influence, just about the right amount of influence, or too little influence (POWER DISCONTENT). Another item asks whether men are better suited for politics. Given that the present study was based on the 1993–1994 NBPS, some potentially useful measures were unavailable.

Socioeconomic Status

Education was measured by number of years completed and coded as such in accordance with a 0 to 1 scale with 1 indicating the highest level of education. Income was measured by one question, "Which of the following income groups includes your total family income in 1992 before taxes?"

Up to $10,000 $30,000–$40,000
$10,000–$15,000 $40,000–$50,000
$15,000–$20,000 $50,000–$75,000
$20,000–$25,000 $75,000 and over
$25,000–$30,000

The coding was from 0 (up to $10,000) to 1 (more than $75,000).

Other Standard Predictors

Church attendance was measured by one question that asked how often the respondent attends religious services. Respondents who indicated never were coded 0. Those who responded once or twice a year were coded .33 and those who responded once or twice a month were coded .66. Finally, respondents who indicated once a week were coded 1. Martial status was also measured by one item, which asked whether the respondent was currently married, widowed, separated, divorced, never been married, or living with a significant other. Respondents who responded married were coded 0, and all others were coded 1. Another item asking the respondent whether he or she lived in a rural or country area, small town, suburb of a city, or in a large city measured urban residence. Respondents who indicated a large city were coded 1. Those who indicated a suburb were coded .75, those who responded a small city were coded .5 and those who responded small town were coded .25. Respondents who indicated rural or country were coded 0. The actual age of respondents at their last birthday was an eight-category variable:

0 = 0–19	.57 = 50–59
.14 = 20–29	.71 = 60–69
.29 = 30–39	.86 = 70–79
.43 = 40–49	1 = 80+

Homeownership was a dichotomous variable coded 1 if the respondent was a homeowner and 0 otherwise.

Analysis & Results

In this analysis, I developed empirical models that captured the effects of individual-level characteristics in addition to race consciousness and black feminist consciousness on black political behavior. A multistage analysis strategy was employed. The first stage involved constructing a scale of political behavior from items available in the 1993–1994 NBPS. The resulting factor was comprised of those questions that measure black political participation. In this analysis, a total of thirteen measures of political behavior were examined.

Table 5.1 reports the results of the factor analysis for political behavior. Factor analysis is a simple way of reducing a large data set into a limited number of "principal components" and the first component typically represents the single best summary of the linear relationship represented in the data. When a set of variables are all positively correlated—as are the thirteen indicators of political behavior used here—the first component represents a general dimension that accounts for more variance in the data as a whole than does any other possible linear combination (Verba and Nie 1972). The first component of black political behavior explains 31 percent of the total variance of the sample and all of the factor loadings were moderate to high, ranging from .345 to .654. More specifically, the VOTING item is the lowest at .345 and the CONTACT PUBLIC OFFICIAL item is the highest at .654. Subsequent

Table 5.1
Political Behavior

	Behavior	Direct	Indirect
VOTING			
PRESIDENTIAL	.345	.103	.610
INDIRECT CONTACT BEHAVIOR			
SIGN PETITION SUPPORTING SOMETHING	.524	.096	.431
SIGN PETITION SUPPORTING CANDIDATE	.567	.262	.391
DIRECT CONTACT BEHAVIOR			
CONTACT PUBLIC OFFICIAL OR AGENCY	.654	−.520	−.030
CONTACT A BLACK ELECTED OFFICIAL	.629	−.564	−.062
CONTACT A WHITE ELECTED OFFICIAL	.595	−.556	−.086
COMMUNAL ACTIVITY			
ATTEND PROTEST MEETING	.583	.128	.140
TAKE PART IN NEIGHBORHOOD MARCH	.438	.251	−.129
CAMPAIGN ACTIVITY			
HELP IN VOTER REGISTRATION DRIVE	.599	.205	−.206
GIVE PEOPLE A RIDE TO THE POLLS			
DONATE MONEY	.381	.296	−.210
ATTEND FUND-RAISER	.626	.213	−.177
HAND OUT CAMPAIGN MATERIAL	.565	.277	−.328

Source: 1993 National Black Politics Study

Eigenvalues = 3.979   1.336   1.022.

Variance = 31%   10%   8%.

components are bipolar, with one set of variables that taps direct contact behavior loading negatively and others loading positively. H̲ second component highlights the best linear combina- e largest amount of residual variance after the effect of mponent has been removed. It is clearly defined by di- behavior. Finally, the third component represents the iance left after the effects of all previous factors of ...nts have been removed. It is clearly defined by political activities that require the least amount of initiative on the part of the citizen—voting and signing petitions. Together, the second and third components explain 18 percent of the total variance of the sample.

The second stage of analysis involved cross-tabulation in an effort to determine whether black political participation differed across gender. For cross-tabulations, the independent variable (gender) represents the column variable (listed across the top), and the dependent variable (political participation) represents the row variable (listed at the left side of the table). In this analysis, the proportion of black women actively engaged in politics was compared to the proportion of black men actively engaged in politics as well (see table 5.2 for the results of this analysis).

In this investigation of the political involvement of black women and men, I consider an array of political activities that require varying degrees of initiative on the part of the citizen to determine whether the level of political involvement differs across gender. The results of this analysis support the proposition that black citizens are more inclined to turn out during an election year. The overwhelming majority (80 percent) of black citizens reported voting in the last presidential election. Of course, this cannot be true of black respondents. Prior research has shown that those who are under special pressure to vote are the ones most likely to misrepresent their behavior when they fail to exercise this right (Bernstein, Chadha, and Montjoy 2001). African Americans in particular are more likely to overreport than whites. Given their long history of exclusion from politics, African Americans are likely to feel guilty when they have failed to vote and it is unlikely that they would confess that guilt during an interview. Another high percentage of black citizens (60 percent of women, 61 percent of men) reported signing a petition in support either of or against something general. Perhaps those who are under special pressure to vote and, for this reason, overreport are just as likely to overstate other modes of behavior when they fail to take full advantage of their democratic rights as citizens. In both instances, the level of participation reported remained virtually the same for black women and men. However, I find that when the definition of political behavior is broadened to include more direct contact behavior, communal and campaign activities, black men are more active in politics than black women.

Table 5.2
Black Political Participation in 1993, Estimated Separately for Gender

	Women N=781	Men N=425	TOTAL N=1,206
VOTING			
PRESIDENTIAL ELECTION	80%	80%	80%
INDIRECT CONTACT BEHAVIOR			
SIGN PETITION IN SUPPORT OF SOMETHING	61	60	60
SIGN PETITION SUPPORTING CANDIDATE	40	45**	41
DIRECT CONTACT BEHAVIOR			
CONTACT PUBLIC OFFICIAL OR AGENCY	32	39**	32
CONTACT BLACK ELECTED OFFICIAL	31	35	32
CONTACT WHITE ELECTED OFFICIAL	21	28**	24
COMMUNAL ACTIVITY			
ATTEND PROTEST MEETING	25	37**	29
TAKE PART IN NEIGHBORHOOD MARCH	20	28**	23
CAMPAIGN ACTIVITY			
HELP IN VOTER REGISTRATION DRIVE	20	28**	23
GIVE PEOPLE A RIDE TO POLLS	23	29**	25
DONATE MONEY	21	30**	24
ATTEND FUND-RAISER	24	33**	27
HAND OUT CAMPAIGN MATERIAL	21	25**	22

Note: Table entries represent percentages.
*$p \le .05$; **$p \le .01$; for 2-tailed test (x^2).

Depicted in table 5.2, the results of this analysis indicate that less than a majority of black citizens (40 percent of women, 45 percent of men) signed a petition in support of a candidate and even fewer contacted a public official or agency (32 percent of women, 39 percent of men), a black elected official (31 percent of women, 35 percent of men), or a white elected official directly (21 percent of women, 28 percent of men). The level of participation declined further when I considered such communal activities as attending a protest meeting (25 percent of women, 37 percent of men) or taking part in a neighborhood march (20 percent of women, 28 percent of men), and such campaign activities as handing out flyers (21 percent of women, 25 percent of men), donating money (21 percent of women, 30 percent of men), attending a fund-raiser (24 percent of women, 33 percent of men), helping in a voter registration drive (20 percent of women, 28 percent of men), and providing transportation to the polls (23 percent of women, 29 percent of men). Statistically significant gender differences were found in relation to signing a petition in support of a candidate, contacting a public official or agency, attending a protest meeting, taking part in a neighborhood march, handing out flyers, donating money, attending a fund-raiser, helping in a voter registration drive, and providing transportation to the polls. Taken together, these results suggest that black men are more politically engaged than black women in both communal and campaign activities. From these data, we see a consistent pattern of dramatic differences between black women and men in their political behavior that is consistent with the literature on the differences in political participation between white women and men (Welch 1977; Beckwith 1986; Clark and Clark 1986; Carroll 1989; Schlozman, Burns, and Verba 1994; Verba, Burns, and Schlozman 1997).

The reason men are more politically engaged than women may be due to social characteristics associated with gender. For example, the masculine advantage when it comes to resources might explain the disparity of engagement. However, Sidney Verba, Nancy Burns, and Kay Schlozman (1997) offer a more detailed explanation by examining men and women in various occupational groups. They point to a difference between men and women in their orientation to politics whereby women are less politically interested, informed, and efficacious than men. They conclude that the lack of resources—money, civic skills, and time—does not fully explain the disparity between the sexes in political participation.

The third stage of analysis involved factor analysis delineating the principal components of race consciousness. It is important to note at this time that the principal components analysis for black feminist consciousness was conducted earlier in chapter 3 and, for this reason, the results do not appear here. All nine of the variables for race consciousness are positively correlated and, as has already been stated, the first component represents a general dimension that accounts for more variance than does any other possible linear combination (Verba and Nie 1972). Depicted in table 5.3, the first component of race consciousness explains 28 percent of the total variance in the sample and all of the factor loadings were moderate to high, ranging from .360 to .607.

Table 5.3
Race Consciousness (RC)

	RC	Blame	Discontent
GROUP IDENTIFICATION			
LINKED FATE WITH BLACKS	.489	.471	.295
SYSTEM BLAME			
UNFAIR OPPORTUNITY	.560	−.128	−.216
UNFAIR DEAL	.493	−.317	.166
SOCIETY UNFAIR	.603	−.471	.219
UNFAIR LEGAL SYSTEM	.607	−.456	.170
POWER DISCONTENT			
ECONOMIC POSITION OF BLACKS	.490	.126	−.639
ECONOMIC POSITION VERSUS WHITES	.604	.190	−.452
COLLECTIVE ACTION			
BLACK MOVEMENT	.514	.426	.347
BLACK ORGANIZATION	.360	.454	.188

Source: 1993 National Black Politics Study.

Eigenvalues = 2.524   1.208   1.006.

Variance =   28%   13%   11%.

The BLACK ORGANIZATION item is the lowest at .360 and the UNFAIR LEGAL SYSTEM item is the highest at .607. Subsequent components are bipolar, with collective action items loading positively and system blame items loading negatively for the second component and power discontent items loading negatively for the third component. Together, these two subsequent components explain 24 percent of the total variance in the sample. Based on the principal components analysis cited here, I conclude that race consciousness is a stable construct that organizes the way black citizens think about political issues affecting their lives in this country.

Table 5.4 presents the estimates for the regression model of overall political behavior separately for black women and men. These findings were quite similar to results reported by Wilcox (1990, 1997). The first important finding is that race consciousness stimulates overall political behavior among black women along with socioeconomic status. More specifically, educational attainment and income have a positive effect on overall political behavior for black women. Rising age and frequency of church attendance were also significant predictors of political behavior for black women. Finally, such predictors of overall political behavior as marital status, home ownership, and urban residence were not significant for black women. Table 5.4 also presents the estimates for the regression model of overall political behavior for black men, and the findings were nearly identical to those aforementioned with one notable exception. In addition to those significant predictors cited above for black female political behavior, home ownership

Table 5.4
Overall Political Behavior Model, Estimated Separately for Gender

Independent Variable	Black Women	Black Men
GROUP CONSCIOUSNESS		
RACE	.401 **	.358 **
	(.051)	(.084)
BLACK FEMINIST	−.037	.025
	(.045)	(.069)
RACE X BLACK FEMINIST	.109	−.357
	(.197)	(.317)
SOCIOECONOMIC STATUS		
EDUCATION	.267 **	.330 **
	(.079)	(.133)
INCOME	.110 **	.171 **
	(.039)	(.065)
OTHER PREDICTORS		
URBAN RESIDENCE	.008	−.009
	(.027)	(.048)
AGE	.131 **	.202 **
	(.036)	(.064)
HOME OWNERSHIP	.006	−.065 *
	(.020)	(.032)
MARITAL STATUS	.008	.004
	(.020)	(.032)
CHURCH ATTENDANCE	.127 **	.109 *
	(.036)	(.055)
CONSTANT	.105	.136
	(.048)	(.088)
ADJUSTED R^2	.227	.169

Source: 1993 National Black Politics Study.

Table entries are unstandardized ordinary least squares regression coefficients, followed by the associated standard error. *p ≤ .05; **p ≤ .01; for 2-tailed test.

was a significant predictor for black male political behavior. Especially striking is the fact that black feminist consciousness does not predict black political behavior for either sex.

Tables 5.5 and 5.6 present the estimates for the regression models of voting, indirect and direct contact behavior, and communal and campaign activity separately for black women and men. My primary interest is testing whether group consciousness and the interaction term consisting of race consciousness and black feminist consciousness are significant predictors of individuals' voting, indirect and direct contact behavior, and communal and campaign activity. The most important finding is that race consciousness is statistically significant for various modes of political behavior with one notable exception. In the case of voting, race consciousness was not statistically significant. The second most important finding is that neither black feminist consciousness nor the interaction term reached statistical significance. Contrary to the hypothesis one might reasonably draw from its conceptualization, black feminist consciousness does not predict voting, indirect and direct contact, and communal and campaign activity among black citizens. Instead, race consciousness seems to constitute the driving force behind active participation in politics. It is important to recognize, however, that these are not competing ideologies. While the interests of women's liberation and black civil rights are sometimes pitted against each other, racism and sexism constitute interlocking systems of oppression that must be combated simultaneously (Robinson 1987; Collins 2000; Gay and Tate 1998; Simien and Clawson 2004).

Black feminist consciousness and the components of race consciousness are complementary approaches to dealing with the oppressive forces that weigh on black people in this country. While there are only a few empirical investigations of this relationship, the existing literature supports the proposition that black feminist consciousness is intertwined with race consciousness (Robinson 1987; Wilcox 1990, 1997; Gay and Tate 1998; Simien and Clawson 2004). Robinson (1987), for example, found a positive association between black feminist consciousness and two components of race consciousness: power discontent and system blame. Similarly, Wilcox (1990) found a positive relationship between feminist consciousness among black women and two components of race consciousness: collective action and system blame. Gay and Tate (1998)

Table 5.5
Modes of Political Behavior, Estimated Separately for Black Women

Independent Variable	Voting	Indirect	Direct	Communal	Campaign
GROUP CONSCIOUSNESS					
RACE	.131	.549 **	.617 **	.428 **	.257 **
	(.090)	(.092)	(.085)	(.084)	(.063)
BLACK FEMINIST	−.038	.001	−.022	−.087	−.043
	(.078)	(.079)	(.074)	(.073)	(.055)
RACE X BLACK FEMINIST	−.658	211	.480	−.065	.060
	(.344)	(.350)	(.325)	(.321)	(.241)
SOCIOECONOMIC STATUS					
EDUCATION	.134	.215	.465 **	.238 **	.217 *
	(.138)	(.140)	(.130)	(.128)	(.097)
INCOME	.173 **	281 *	.073	−.056	.109*
	(.069)	(.070)	(.065)	(.064)	(.048)
OTHER PREDICTORS					
URBAN RESIDENCE	−.011	.083	.043	.045	−.051
	(.047)	(.048)	(.044)	(.044)	(.033)
AGE	.281 **	.134 **	.230 **	.006	.088*
	(.063)	(.064)	(.059)	(.059)	(.044)
HOME OWNERSHIP	.003	−.032	.023	.003	.015
	(.035)	(.035)	(.033)	(.032)	(.024)
MARITAL STATUS	−.028	.017	.004	.004	.017
	(.035)	(.035)	(.033)	(.032)	(.024)
CHURCH ATTENDANCE	.193 **	.083	.073	.150	.157 **
	(.063)	(.064)	(.060)	(.059)	(.044)
CONSTANT	.632 **	.174	−.097	.002	−.073
	(.084)	(.086)	(.080)	(.090)	(.059)
ADJUSTED R^2	.087	.153	.178	.061	.106

Source: 1993 National Black Politics Study.

Table entries are unstandardized ordinary least squares regression coefficients, followed by the associated standard error. *p ≤ .05; **p ≤ .01; for 2-tailed test.

also discovered a positive relationship between gender identification and race identification whereby gender identification enhanced the effect of race identification on five policy issues: busing for integration, affirmative action, food stamps spending, spending on schools, and Medicare spending. Simien and Clawson (2004) have since demonstrated that a commitment to black feminist principles does not

Table 5.6
Modes of Political Behavior, Estimated Separately for Black Men

Independent Variable	Voting	Indirect	Direct	Communal	Campaign
GROUP CONSCIOUSNESS					
RACE	.147	.430 **	.456 **	.424 **	.288 **
	(.131)	(.138)	(.132)	(.128)	(.109)
BLACK FEMINIST	.166	−.104	.062	.154	−.027
	(.107)	(.113)	(.108)	(.105)	(.089)
RACE X BLACK FEMINIST	.310	−.378	−.467	.484	−.754
	(.496)	(.522)	(.499)	(.485)	(.411)
SOCIOECONOMIC STATUS					
EDUCATION	.122	.073	.776 **	.308	.218
	(.207)	(.219)	(.209)	(.203)	(.172)
INCOME	.123	.303 **	.184	.036	.172*
	(.102)	(.107)	(.103)	(.100)	(.085)
OTHER PREDICTORS					
URBAN RESIDENCE	.000	−.020	−.025	.112	−.048
	(.074)	(.078)	(.075)	(.073)	(.062)
AGE	.311 **	.073	.250 **	.052	.265 **
	(.100)	(.105)	(.100)	(.098)	(.083)
HOME OWNERSHIP	.046	−.129 **	−.054	−.063	−.072
	(.051)	(.053)	(.051)	(.049)	(.042)
MARITAL STATUS	−.069	−.118	−.013	−.023	.047
	(.049)	(.052)	(.050)	(.048)	(.041)
CHURCH ATTENDANCE	.084	−.078	.161	−180 *	−.165*
	(.086)	(.090)	(.086)	(.084)	(.071)
CONSTANT	.531 **	.378 **	−.118	−.043	.115
	(.137)	(.145)	(.138)	(.147)	(.114)
ADJUSTED R^2	.064	.064	.158	.095	.081

Source: 1993 National Black Politics Study.

Table entries are unstandardized ordinary least squares regression coefficients, followed by the associated standard error. *p < .05; **p < .01; for 2-tailed test.

detract from racial solidarity. They conclude that black men and women have similar levels of black feminist consciousness and its effect on black attitudes toward affirmative action and abortion were fairly comparable across gender. Finally, I (Simien 2005) have shown that support for the women's movement, once seen as a threat to the political cohesiveness of black people in the United States, helped further the sense of race identification among African Americans. While all of these researchers maintain that the two reinforce and facilitate one another, they also acknowledge that many black women feel pressured to prioritize race over gender. The fact is many "black women will support their interests as women, but their support can be muted and even overwhelmed" when those interests collide with race. Black women who fail to subordinate their interests as women are made to feel disloyal to the race (Gay and Tate 1998, 183). That is to say, race consciousness wipes out the effects of black feminist consciousness in determining black political behavior because these two constructs are closely related to one another.

Given that the core themes of black feminist consciousness emphasize the importance of political activism, a particularly interesting finding was that black feminist consciousness did not predict communal behavior. In this analysis, communal behavior was limited to taking part in a neighborhood march and attending a protest meeting. As shown by Sidney Verba, Kay Schlozman, Henry Brady, and Norman Nie (1995), the civic volunteerism model demonstrates that both the motivation and capacity to participate in politics have their roots in nonpolitical institutions that lay the foundation for future political involvement and provide opportunities for the acquisition of relevant resources. For example, the black church is well-known for its involvement in politics. It provides the institutional infrastructure for political mobilization and offers opportunities for members of the congregation to develop skills that are relevant for politics (Tate 1991; Calhoun-Brown 1999; Harris 1999). Considering that communal behavior was defined by merely two political activities, this seems to suggest that an expanded model of communal behavior inclusive of nonpolitical activities might yield different results. Thus, black feminist consciousness and its effect on communal behavior warrant further investigation.

Other independent variables were associated with voting, indirect and direct contact, and communal and campaign activity. There were identical results for campaign activity where race consciousness, and socioeconomic status, age, and church attendance reached statistical significance for both sexes. However, the effects of group consciousness and socioeconomic status, along with other predictors, such as age, urban residence, marital status, home ownership, and church attendance, on the various modes of political behavior often differed across gender.

Conclusion

This chapter began with a discussion of Mary Church Terrell, providing context for the analysis cited here. Toward the latter part of her life, Terrell shifted her tactics from pursuing interracial understanding through journalism and speeches to nonviolent direct action through economic boycotts, lunch counter sit-ins, and protest marches. Using a variety of political acts beyond voting, she multiplied her political effectiveness and communicated more precise messages to policymakers by attacking racial and sexual discrimination in three areas: the courts, the streets, and Congress. In light of this, she set out to influence judicial decisions, policy outputs, and legislative statutes.

Terrell, for example, applied for membership in the Washington, D.C., chapter of the American Association of University Women. In 1946, the board of directors rejected her request. However, after a three-year court battle, she was admitted to the local chapter in Washington, D.C., and the National Association of University Women voted to admit members regardless of race. At the same time, Terrell lobbied Congress for passage of the Equal Rights Amendment. In 1950, she marched with a cane at the head of a picket line to desegregate local stores and restaurants in our nation's capital (Sterling 1979; B. Jones 1990; Mullane 1993). Terrell then spearheaded a letter-writing campaign and solicited support from civic and social organizations as well as high-profile government officials. The tactics of picketing and boycotting, in addition to the distribution of flyers and leaflets, were instrumental to the success of this movement in Washington, D.C.

It is my view that democratic principles come alive only when people like Mary Church Terrell participate in American political processes. Undoubtedly, Terrell took her role as a citizen of the United States seriously. Today, when far fewer citizens take advantage of their democratic rights, Terrell stands out as a role model we all can follow. Only one-half of Americans vote in presidential elections, and only one-third vote in congressional elections. Even fewer vote in local elections. Roughly one-tenth of the population takes full advantage of opportunities to participate in campaigns (Verba, Schlozman et al. 1995; Rosenston, and Hansen 1993). Activists who give money to candidates, help in voter registration drives, distribute campaign material, write letters to legislators, attend protest rallies, and join civic organizations are rare. One enduring explanation for this phenomenon is that political participation is class based: people who participate tend to have more resources and come from the upper echelon of society. In other words, citizens who actively participate in politics differ from those who do not in terms of demographic characteristics—most notably, socioeconomic status (Verba, Schlozman et al. 1993). Mary Church Terrell is one prime example.

This research is the first to examine the overall impact of two models—socioeconomic status and group consciousness—on black political behavior, including *both* race consciousness *and* black feminist consciousness under the rubric of group consciousness. The results of this analysis reveal that race consciousness is significantly related to black political behavior. More specifically, black citizens who recognize that their individual life chances are inextricably tied to the race, express awareness that structural barriers rather than personal failings account for the subordinate status of the race, report disenchantment with status deprivation, and exhibit a commitment to group strategies in confronting racism are more likely to actively participate in politics than those who do not subscribe to the core beliefs cited above. At the same time, this analysis reveals that black political behavior is not influenced by black feminist consciousness. While many black women possess a sense of race and gender consciousness derived from their unique disadvantaged status and many black men are cognizant of and sympathetic toward the particular predicament of black women, both black women and men recognize the overwhelming importance of race loyalty. Knowing that the black feminist camp has always argued that feminist consciousness and race consciousness go hand in hand, it is essential to point out that the central notion of black feminist consciousness focuses on the ways in which "isms" work together to dominate certain groups. Intersectionality, as it has already been defined, suggests that the way to deal with interlocking systems of oppression is to approach them as a problem that must be addressed simultaneously. Thus, it is consistent with the underpinnings of black feminist consciousness that race consciousness would be closely associated with it.

It is also worth noting that black political behavior is influenced by socioeconomic status (i.e., education and income). Education is the strongest predictor of political behavior and there is an increase in political behavior as education rises. The findings on income and political behavior reveal that rising income is associated with increased activity in politics. Black men are also more likely to participate than black women when considering various modes of political behavior. Of course, this finding deserves further investigation to better understand how the political system structures opportunities for black women and men to actively participate in politics. In short, there are clear and apparent gender differences in black political behavior worth examining in further detail.

Chapter Six

THE FUTURE OF FEMINIST SCHOLARSHIP AND BLACK POLITICS RESEARCH

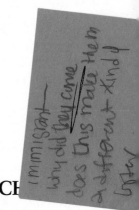

A fact worthy of note is that in every reform in which the Negro woman has taken part, during the past fifty-years, she has been as aggressive, progressive and dependable as those who inspired the reform or led it.

—Nannie Helen Burroughs,
"Black Women and Reform"

From 1900 to 1960, Nannie Helen Burroughs challenged the hierarchal practices and religiously sanctioned rules that effectively silenced black women's voices and accentuated their subordinate status vis-à-vis men in the National Baptist Convention—the largest black religious organization. In 1900, Burroughs delivered a speech at the annual meeting of the National Baptist Convention identifying many of the real and symbolic barriers that black male clergy sought to impose on black women in the church. Her speech, "How the Sisters Are Hindered from Helping," contested the silent helpmate image of women in the church and led to the formation of the Women's Convention Auxiliary, which continues to function to this day as a component of the National Baptist Convention. The existence of this separate, autonomous space allowed black churchwomen to culminate their religious activities at the state and local level by electing their own leaders, developing their own agenda, and governing their own members (Higginbotham 1993). Members of the Women's Convention Auxiliary continue to see themselves as part of an evangelical sisterhood.

119

Nannie Helen Burroughs is perhaps best known for advocating women's political leadership in the church and equal educational opportunities for girls in the larger society. In 1908, she proposed that a special Sunday be designated "National Women's Day" as a way to formally recognize the contributions made by African American women in religious circles. On this day, women lead and speak in the worship service of Baptist churches across the country. Since its inception, National Women's Day has grown to encompass a series of events, including a meal served to women by men of the church. In 1909, Burroughs established a training school for women and girls so as to increase their employability in our nation's capital. With the help and support of the Women's Convention Auxiliary, the school opened its doors and offered missionary as well as industrial training that prepared women for jobs as cooks, nurses, clerks, housekeepers, stenographers, and dressmakers. The school addressed the reality of job discrimination and the need for low-status black women to be self-sufficient wage earners by professionalizing domestic service (Higginbotham 1993).

The National Training School, as its name implies, regulated the manners of the students and served a disciplining function. Students were evaluated on their personal cleanliness and neatness as well as politeness and respectability. Given the disciplinary nature of the school and its deliberate emphasis on domestic service, Burroughs was sometimes called "Mrs. Booker T. Washington" and dubbed the "female Booker T. Washington" because the curriculum of the National Training School resembled that of the Tuskegee Institute founded by Washington (Harley 1996). While the women of Tuskegee received similar academic preparatory work in domestic service and the institute stressed self-sufficiency just as the National Training School did, Nannie Helen Burroughs has yet to receive nearly as much scholarly attention as Booker T. Washington. To be marginalized in this way is especially unfortunate, considering that her ideas about industrial education and vocational training mirrored those of Washington. With her criticism of the National Baptist Convention and stormy relationship with ministerial alliances, she exhibited the same courage and principled convictions of Ida B. Wells-Barnett and Maria W. Stewart (Hine 1993; Harley 1996; Gilkes 2001). Like Mary Church Terrell, Burroughs headed a major women's organization, being president of the Women's Convention Auxiliary. In these ways, Nannie Helen Burroughs resembled past reformers as she awakened the consciousness of black churchwomen and sparked a women's movement within the National Baptist Convention.

This concluding chapter is as much about the forces that prevent Anna Julia Cooper, Ida B. Wells-Barnett, Maria W. Stewart, Mary Church Terrell, and Nannie Helen Burroughs from figuring more prominently in history as it is about the forces that discourage the study of black feminist voices in political science. Here, I suggest that black women intellectuals in general and black female political scientists in particular are crucial to broadening the scope of feminist scholarship and black politics research. As stated earlier, the purpose of this book is to pave the way for an impressive and compelling agenda that advances the study of African American women within the discipline of political science. In prior chapters, I discussed the literature on black feminist consciousness, its determinants, and its overall impact on political behavior. In this concluding chapter, I set out to do three things. First, I review the findings of previous chapters and discuss their contribution to the extant literature. Second, I assess the limitations of the data and methodology used here. Third, I consider what the findings in this book mean for the future of feminist scholarship and black politics research.

Summary and Review of Findings

In chapter 1, black feminist consciousness was defined as the recognition that African American women are status deprived because they must face discrimination on the basis of both their race and their gender. This definition implied that many black women readily recognize disadvantage and discrimination due to their unique disadvantaged status in the United States and that many black men are cognizant of and sympathetic toward the particular predicament of black women because both sexes experience day-to-day encounters with class exploitation and race oppression. With this definition, I pulled together so much of what was a murky mire of assumptions and cleared away a lot of the underbrush of popular discourse so prevalent around issues of black feminist sentiments, cross-pressures, and the hierarchy of interests by identifying the underlying themes that delineate the contours of black feminist consciousness.

The first theme, intersectionality, suggests that interlocking oppressions circumscribe the lives of black women through day-to-day encounters with race and gender oppression (Crenshaw 1993, 1995; D. King 1988). Intersectionality involves an acute sense of awareness that black women "don't have the luxury of choosing to fight only one battle" because they must contend with multiple, interlocking systems of oppression and the actuality of layered experiences is multiplicative as opposed to additive (T. Jones 2000, 56). The second theme emphasizes the struggle to eliminate patriarchy in all aspects of black life. It is the acceptance of the belief that gender inequality exists within the black community and beyond. The third theme maintains that feminism benefits the black community by challenging patriarchy as an institutionalized oppressive structure and advocating the building of coalitions to further the cause of equality and justice for women. The fourth theme suggests that a sense of belonging or conscious loyalty to the group in question (i.e., black women) stems from lived experiences, specifically day-to-day encounters with race, class, and gender oppression (D. King 1988; Guy-Sheftall 1995). In other words, the individual who identifies with the group label comes to realize that individual life chances are inextricably tied to the group and that collective action is a necessary form of resistance (Dawson 1994). In short, scholars have emphasized four themes that delineate the contours of black feminist consciousness: intersectionality, gender (in) equality, benefits of black feminism for the black community, and linked fate with black women.

To date, political scientists have utilized two empirical approaches to study gender-related consciousness among black women. First, scholars have used items designed to tap feminist consciousness among white women to measure black feminist consciousness. This approach is problematic because it assumes that black feminism and white feminism are comparable. There are many differences, both historically and in contemporary times, between the ways in which black women and white women experience sexism in this country. Thus, I argue that survey items designed with white women in mind result in a measurement of support for white feminism—not black feminist consciousness. Second, researchers have measured gender identification and race identification and then used the interaction of these two variables to create a measure of black feminist consciousness. This approach is problematic because it assumes that race and gender are separate, unrelated categories. If race and gender are conceived as separate constructs, there can be no account of how attitudes may change as a result of cross-pressures to subordinate the interests of women for the sake of protecting black men from racism. Thus, I argue that using the interaction of these two variables fails to capture the simultaneity of oppression.

In chapter 2, I contended that the dominant conceptualization of group consciousness had been ineffective in articulating the politicized group identification of black women because race and gender have been treated as unrelated categories. The substantive question addressed in this chapter focused on ways in which black women had been theoretically erased from the literature on race and gender-related consciousness. That is, how has the absence of black feminist voices impaired our understanding of group consciousness? Citing evidence and examples, I answered this question directly by making the case for the inclusion of survey items that address the commitment to activism among black feminists, assess the politicized identification with black women, and capture issues of discrimination that black women face in the home, the workplace, and the dominant society.

In "Measuring Feminist Consciousness," Cook (1989) combined the feeling thermometer rating for the women's liberation movement with the "close to women" item in an effort to tap gender consciousness. In her analysis, women who did not express closeness to other women were coded as lacking gender consciousness. Those who felt close to other women, but rated the women's movement 50 degrees or less were also coded as having low gender consciousness. Using a similar approach, Conover (1988) drew insight from a "women-centered perspective" and focused on the extent to which women identified themselves as homemakers. In her analysis, she combined the feeling thermometer rating for feminists with the homemaker item in order to tap feminist identity. To establish validity for this measure, she examined the relationship between feminist identity and other criterion variables: feeling thermometer ratings for women, the women's movement, and the women's liberation movement.

In both instances, Cook (1989) and Conover (1988) overlooked the full array of factors that thwarted a formidable interracial women's alliance and led black women to organize around their own interests. For decades, the women's liberation movement reflected white middle-class bias in its objectives and aims (Fulenwider 1980; hooks 1981; A. Davis 1984). Its membership and leadership treated the interest of black women as secondary to their own by excluding them from the movement's agenda. In addition, the traditional housewife model has never fit most African American women (M. King 1975; Stone 1979; D. King 1988; Guy-Sheftall 1995; Collins 2000). African American women are more likely to be heads of households, historically their labor participation has exceeded that of white women, and they usually possess more decision-making authority in their parental and conjugal roles (M. King 1975; Stone 1979; D. King 1988; Prestage 1991; Guy-Sheftall 1995). Without much choice in the matter, African American women have worked at higher rates than white women because their families have been burdened by family-income inequality and two incomes are necessary for familial economic survival. Even today, these factors would likely influence feeling thermometer ratings for the women's liberation movement and responses to the homemaker item by black women. However, there is yet another factor that has made it difficult to detect whether black women develop gender-related consciousness.

It is the case that many "black women will support their interests as women, but their support can be muted and even overwhelmed" when those interests collide with race because the hierarchy of interest within the black community assigns priority to race over gender (Gay and Tate 1998, 183). Again and again the need for unity has been misnamed as a need for homogeneity (Stone 1979; Robinson 1987; B. Smith 1995). The relationship between the entire community and the interests of its female members is well understood and creates a powerful dynamic in which black women must subordinate matters of vital concern to them for the sake of protecting black men (Lorde 1984; B. Smith 1995; Jordan 1997). The political logic is that black men must be protected from the forces of racism first and foremost. This relationship accounts for differences between black women and men in their beliefs toward gender equality and feminist priorities as they appear in final factor solutions cited here.

Chapter 3 described how I empirically measured black feminist consciousness. It included a detailed description of the data set, variable measures, and analysis strategy. Through the use of factor analysis and bivariate correlations, I developed and validated a measure of black feminist consciousness—that alone being a significant contribution. The distinctions between black feminist consciousness and feminist consciousness were systematically investigated. As I have shown, black feminist consciousness and feminist consciousness are two separate constructs. But this is only half of the story.

Factor analysis delineated the principal components of black feminist consciousness for black women and men separately. The results of this analysis indicated that both black women and men experience some sense of internal conflict when considering the "both movements" item. It is believed that the "both movements" item was the most difficult for respondents to answer because this item activates the sense of internal conflict often experienced by black women when they feel that they must choose between race and gender. The "both movements" item captures this sense of internal conflict by forcing respondents to considering whether African American women suffered from both sexism within the black movement and racism within the women's movement or whether black women suffer from mostly the same problems as black men. In this instance, the hierarchy of interests did not produce the same divisive outcome for black men as it did for black women. The second dimension of the factor analysis for black feminist consciousness was clearly associated with the "both movements" item for black men.

While it appears that black feminist consciousness is quite widespread among black women and men, it is the case that black men are equally and, in some instances, more likely to support black feminist principles. When we examine just those who "strongly agree" with the position that there should be more black women clergy, a twelve-point difference exists between black women and men. Despite the significance of this finding, the question that remains unanswered is whether black men have truly progressed in their thinking of traditional gender roles. It is no secret that the black church has played a preeminent role in inhibiting the development of black feminist consciousness (Stone 1979; Harris 1999). For this reason, I turned to another data set with alternative questions that made more of a distinction between black women and men. The purpose was to determine whether these results (particularly the equal likelihood of black men and women advocating the black feminist agenda) reflected the type of questions asked more than the reality or the ingenuity of black men to respond with political correct answers.

Using data from the 1984–1988 NBES, I found that there was a significant difference in the responses to three items by black women and men. One item asked respondents whether men were better suited emotionally for politics. Another asked whether men and women possess too much influence, just about the right amount of influence, or too little influence. The results of this analysis indicated that roughly 39 percent of black women strongly disagree with the statement that men are better suited for politics, versus 27 percent of black men. And while fewer than one-half of the male respondents (45 percent) indicated that men have too much power, the majority of women (60 percent) indicated that men did in fact possess too much power. Finally, one-third of black women (30 percent) believed that women have far too little power, in contrast with one-quarter of black men (24 percent). Of course, these items do not capture the full essence of black feminist thought. However, they do capture some component of feminism.

Chapter 4 examined the determinants of black feminist consciousness for both black women and men. Wilcox (1990, 1997) has described black women who support feminist ideals as young, well educated, employed with relatively high incomes, and race conscious. The demographic analysis of black feminist consciousness that I presented was consistent with much of the literature on feminist consciousness. Race identification and education were the best predictors of black feminist consciousness, followed by age, power discontent, and income for black women. In contrast with the literature, marital status, employment status, and urban residence were not significant predictors of black feminist consciousness for black women. The roles of black women and white women differ appreciably. There are many differences both historically and in contemporary times in the ways in which black and white women experience sexism in this country. It is likely that black women reach full actualization of black feminist consciousness through day-to-day encounters with race and gender oppression, whether they be working or not, married or not, and residing in the big city or a rural community. Entirely absent from the literature is information on the determinants of black feminist consciousness for black men. As I have shown, race identification and income were the best predictors of black feminist consciousness, followed by interviewer sex for black men.

In chapter 5, I assessed the overall impact of two models— socioeconomic status and group consciousness—on black political behavior. I found that there were statistically significant gender differences in political behavior in relation to communal and campaign activity: where black males were more politically engaged than their black female counterparts. Especially striking was the fact that black feminist consciousness did not predict black political behavior. Perhaps the positive relationship between race consciousness and black feminist consciousness explains this phenomenon. The unexpected failure of black feminist consciousness to produce a positive effect on political behavior necessitates further examination of the meaning of black feminist consciousness. Of course, there are a few possible reasons why black feminist consciousness was not a significant predictor for black political behavior: measurement error in the independent variable, operationalization of the dependent variable, or model misspecification.

Limitations of the Data and Future Research

No matter how sophisticated the statistical technique used to estimate black political behavior, a model that fails to include all relevant variables consistently leads to biased results that purportedly apply to all African Americans without careful attention paid to male and female members of the race as well as the poor working-class and the wealthy middle-class for which there is a growing divide within black communities (Wilson 1998; Harris-Lacewell 2003). Failing to account for other mediating factors such as political trust and efficacy similarly leads to conclusions based on incomplete (or inaccurate) information. Future research must account more fully for the effects of psychological involvement—trust in government, public engagement, and political efficacy at both the individual and group level— on various modes of political behavior, not just voter turnout (see, for example, Mangum 2003).

Given that black women are expected to be found among the least likely of voters because they lack the necessary resources for active participation in politics, future research might test whether lower levels of trust in government and lower levels of political efficacy encourage their increased rate of participation across various modes. In 1981, Baxter and Lansing found that black women reported the lowest levels of trust in government and the lowest feelings of political efficacy as compared to other race-sex groups. However, they voted at higher rates than black men, and the gap in voting between black women and men was less than the gap for whites (Baxter and Lansing 1981; Prestage 1991; Harmon-Martin 1994). This would appear counterintuitive, but prior research has indicated that the most active blacks are "politically discontented," exhibiting a combination of low levels of trust in government and low levels of political efficacy (Baxter and Lansing 1981; Ardrey 1994). In fact, Saundra Ardrey (1994) called for a reexamination of the hypothesized relationship that exists between low levels of trust and efficacy because heightened participation on the part of black women could be interpreted as political savvy. The idea is that if you distrust a political figure, one way to keep that person "honest" and accountable is to actively engage in the electoral process.

No items were available that tapped such important feminist concerns as paid maternity leave, federally subsidized child care, sexual harassment, welfare reform, subsidized abortions, and equal pay for comparable worth. These issues constitute those about which feminist organizations have lobbied and, as a result, received a good deal of media attention. In organizing to promote these concerns, feminist organizations create a network of complementary alliances. Both white and black feminist organizations have been active in the policymaking process, specializing in research and constituency development for many years. Still, they must continue to develop strategies to create strong bonds, raise awareness, and link consciousness to collective action among potential and active members. By now, it is well-known that feminist organizations experienced problems recruiting and mobilizing black women because the movement for women's rights was driven by the aims and objectives of white middle-class women who treated the interests of black women as secondary to their own. Choosing not to participate in the white-dominated mainstream feminist organizations, many black women formed their own organizations—namely, the National Black Feminist Organization and the Third World Women's Alliance (Roth 2004).

Given the emphasis many white feminists place on building coalitions with black feminists today, future research must meet their need to pursue activist strategies and policy goals that appeal to black women. One such policy goal might be welfare reform as contemporary feminists argue with detailed data and intense passion that mothers on welfare (a disproportionate number of whom are African American) are not adequately served by welfare to work programs as they exist in the United States when their needy children often suffer from abuse and neglect (Sidel 1996; Roberts 2002). More work must be done to develop survey items that measure a behavioral commitment to grassroots activism and multiracial coalitions among those who support gender equality and feminist priorities from both the lower and upper echelons of society. A behavioral commitment refers to a belief that one ought to engage in collective action that will challenge patriarchy as an institutionalized oppressive structure. It is this component of black feminist consciousness that was not available in the 1993–1994 NBPS. Such items would make it easier for researchers to separate those with a genuine commitment to black feminism from those with merely a fleeting recognition of the discrimination faced by black women. I am concerned that current items may be "too easy" for black respondents.

In several high-profile cases that pitted the interests of black women and black men against one another, many in the black community lined up on the side of black men, yet my data reveal high levels of support for black feminist consciousness. Perhaps the 1993–1994 NBPS does not set the bar high enough. To be sure, further research on black feminist consciousness must be done and another national survey of African Americans must be conducted, allowing us to improve the measure of black feminist consciousness.

No items were available that assessed gender role socialization for either black women or men. Future empirical investigations of black feminist consciousness should examine intragroup differences with special attention paid to gender role socialization and class-based differences in attitudes toward gender equality and feminist priorities. Another national survey of African Americans might focus on how messages of gender role socialization are transmitted from mother to daughter as well as from father to son and how such information influences the development of black feminist consciousness. Given that income was a significant predictor of black feminist consciousness for both sexes, this focus would result in better models of black feminist support and predict the conditions under which black feminists of all classes and both sexes might support a multiracial alliance to end patriarchy.

No items were available to differentiate between people of African descent who identify themselves as black feminists, as womanists, as both, or in some cases as neither, preferring the term "Africana womanists." Far from being merely a superficial or elitist exercise, the act of self-naming is important because it creates community while signaling potential alliances and highlighting fixed priorities. Africana womanism represents a distinct ideology that differs from feminism in general and black feminism in particular. An Afrocentric theory, it builds on a basic master narrative about the nature and origins of feminism. Africana womanists, such as Clenora Hudson-Weems, reject feminism as an alien ideology derived from the historical and cultural experiences of white middle-class women. On this basis, Africana womanists provide a scathingly provocative critique of feminists in general and black feminists in particular so as to purposely distance themselves from these respective camps. They set themselves apart by declaring other forms of black antisexist thought as less authentic, counterfeit—that is, white feminism in black face. Africana womanists insist that a black antisexist politics cannot be too closely aligned with the feminist movement and so black feminists are thought to follow a template and model themselves after mainstream feminist organizations driven by the aims and objectives of white middle-class women.

While it would be tempting to dismiss this theory as a relic of black political thought from the 1970s, Africana womanism demands further investigation as it has garnered support from the most prominent wing of Black or Africana Studies—that is, black nationalists. First and foremost, scholars must begin to take seriously the function of self-definition in developing critical social theory. While Africana womanism's affiliation with nationalism exaggerates out-group differences and minimizes in-group variation by assuming a stable and homogenous racial group identity, black feminism's connection with women's liberation both domestically and globally cultivates its rejection on the grounds that feminism is perceived as a for-whites-only affair. Africana womanists' efforts to distance themselves ideologically from feminists in general and black feminists in particular are endemic to the process of building anti-sexist theory and engaging in meaningful praxis—that is, lack of consensus and divergent interests that naturally splinter groups into respective factions. Second, Africana womanism must be assessed in terms of its practical implications for coalition politics, issue advocacy networks, and constituency development. Given that the ideological priorities of Africana womanism resonate with black public opinion today, feminists in general and black feminists in particular must develop ways of fomenting and implementing coalition politics that counter the rank ordering of race, class, and gender as separate constructs. Future research must therefore determine the extent to which black feminists, as compared to Africana womanists, have been successful at mobilizing a mass following and transmitting their beliefs about the matrix of domination. That is to say, insufficient attention has been paid to investigating divergent ideological dispositions and competing interests as expressed by subpopulations within black communities—in this case, those who self-identify as black feminists and Africana womanists.

Practical Implications

In recent years, the federal government has changed "welfare as we know it" and politicians have pledged "no child shall be left behind" in states where cash assistance to families with needy children have been either reduced or eliminated altogether. While several feminists have objected to the devaluation of women's work in the home and campaigned for sufficient jobs with adequate wages as well as child-care services that would accommodate employment, the federal government has responded with welfare reform programs that force single mothers to replace their monthly checks with either a low wage job or a husband (Hartman 1989; Naples 1998; Roberts 2002). Whether this reform constitutes a real solution to the problem of "welfare dependency" hinges on the success rates of its recipients on public assistance to secure jobs that allow them to pull their families out of poverty. At the heart of this debate about welfare reform lies the question, Are work mandates combined with skills training and other employment-related services helping single mothers find jobs, earn decent salaries, and take better care of their children?

Given the emphasis on "expert knowledge" and the rise of a technocratic class in this complex information age, debates over welfare reform and its effectiveness often take place between and among highly educated elites working for various public agencies, research foundations (or think tanks), public lobbying associations, and legislators in Washington, D.C., and across the country. Both policy specialists and research analysts evaluate the performance and rate the effectiveness of work-related activities and specific work programs in light of their costs to the federal government and benefits to the public at large without much input from those who participate in the programs. In this way, trained experts influence governmental decision-making and promote technical solutions to emerging societal problems by virtue of their specialized knowledge and position in administrative settings within dominant political and economic institutions where they are typically shielded from public scrutiny (Fischer 1990). For this reason, it is especially important for feminists—both black and white—to pursue mutually reinforcing social reform efforts and political protest activities that unite low-income, working-class mothers, prospective mothers, and highly educated professionals for whom motherhood outside of marriage is sometimes a deliberate alternative lifestyle choice so as to engage women of all classes in grassroots organizing, activist mothering, and community work alongside and on behalf of the most vulnerable to oppression (Sidel 1996; Wing 1997; Naples 1998; Roberts 2002). Such advocacy networks would improve the material conditions of welfare recipients, influence government policymaking and public attitudes toward poverty, and demonstrate the assertiveness and potential of poor working-class women to form political alliances with upper-middle-class career women (Wilson 1998; Springer 1999; Roberts 2002).

To realize this objective, both individual and organized feminists must place higher priority on collective action and support policy goals that transcend the experiences of individual women on welfare with the purpose of establishing strong, universal programs that reduce poverty by raising the minimum wage, providing high-quality subsidized child care, and increasing the supply of affordable housing for both single-parent and two-parent households (Orfield and Ashkinaze 1991; Sidel 1996; Wilson 1996, 1998; Roberts 2002). That is to say, those genuinely committed to feminist principles must form a network of complementary alliances so as to combine their efforts and support economic policies that benefit the poor and working classes, in which women of all races are disproportionately represented in the United States. Recognizing the need and potential for mutually reinforcing social reform efforts, activists of all races and both sexes might begin to focus more on the interests they hold in common versus the differences that jeopardize their success as a formidable political alliance.

Alternative Approaches

Given that the present study assumed that traditional mainstream political practices were appropriate yardsticks against which to measure black political behavior, and the finding that black feminist consciousness failed to have a positive effect on various modes of political behavior, it is quite possible that the exclusive focus on traditional mainstream political practices such as electoral and protest activities obscured the reality. Historically, women's community-based activities have involved both paid and unpaid work in churches, schools, child-care programs, hospitals, and recreation centers in their efforts to facilitate grassroots campaigns for social justice (Naples 1998). Perhaps the ability to think more broadly about what constitutes political behavior would aid our understanding of black feminism and its overall impact on various

modes of political behavior by enabling the researcher to pose new
questions and take into account community action on the grassroots level. It is the case that African Americans use a variety of
nonorganizational strategies to challenge interlocking systems of
oppression (Kelley 1994; Naples 1998; Mattis 2001). These strategies of resistance include selective use of consumer dollars, workplace sabotage, talking back to authority, and quitting at times
that are inconvenient for employers (Mattis 2001). In short, a
broader focus on a range of organized as well as individual-level
political behaviors might yield more accurate findings.

In future analyses of various modes of political behavior,
scholars might privilege African American women's specific conceptualizations about the causes of race and sex discrimination
and their ideas about the most effective strategies for combating
the simultaneity of oppression. Survey researchers and public opinion scholars must develop measures of political behavior that are
reflective of the particularized experiences and goals of black communities, which means broadening our view of legitimate political
acts for African Americans in general and African American
women in particular. Such survey items might address the commitment to grassroots activism among black feminists, determine
whether a politicized identification with black women makes one
more loyal to black civil rights than women's liberation, and consider issues of discrimination that black women face in the home,
the workplace, and the dominant society so as to explain labor
market outcomes and work–family values. The bottom line is this:
the conceptualization of black political behavior must be determined, in part, by an appreciation of the lived experience and the
political objectives of both African American women and men.

Perhaps the most useful approach to the study of black feminism and political behavior would be one that examines individual
and institutional activism in the context of shifting political, historical, and material conditions for African Americans in general
and African American women in particular (Mattis 2001). More
specifically, scholars might situate black political behavior in a
context relative to the government's role in political socialization
and individual motivations for active participation in social reform
efforts. For example, African American women's political activism
within the modern civil rights movement has not been accurately

documented, but rather conveniently forgotten. African American women were instrumental to the civil rights movement in their roles as organizers, fund-raisers, and bridge leaders on the local level (Robnett 1997; Collier-Thomas and Franklin 2001; Ling and Monteith 2004). Nonetheless, African American women were typically shunned as public spokespersons for the movement and high-profile leadership positions were reserved for African American men. As long as social scientists in general and political scientists in particular continue to ignore or mischaracterize African American women as helpmates on the sidelines versus leaders on the frontlines, our understanding of the modern civil rights movement will remain incomplete and hopelessly inaccurate when African Americans are presented as a largely monolithic group despite different movement experiences determined by race, sexuality, class, and gender dynamics (Simien 2003).

It is in this regard that the life of Fannie Lou Hamer, field secretary for the Student Nonviolent Coordinating Committee and cofounder of the Mississippi Freedom Democratic Party, becomes illustrative. Despite orchestrating tremendously successful grassroots campaigns that advanced black liberation and attested to her leadership capabilities, Hamer was typically shunned as a public spokesperson for the modern civil rights movement by members of the college-educated, professional segment of the African American community. At a time when feminine respectability was widely accepted as a vitally important tool of protest, Hamer refused to downplay her activist credentials and conform to middle-class standards when she lacked the necessary status indicators for elite group membership (Ling and Monteith 2004). Such class-specific classifications as social refinement and artistic sensibility were beyond her grasp, especially when considering Hamer dropped out of school at the age of twelve, worked full time as a sharecropper on a rural plantation, and lived in a small frame house with no running water (Mills 1994; Lee 1999). Her speech pattern was characterized by the use of multiple and double negatives, several forms of the verb and auxiliary *be,* and distinct pronunciations that violated the norms of standard American English. Given her unfeminine militancy, the upper echelon of black civil society recoiled from supporting her as they subscribed to conventional notions of respectability for women (Ling and Monteith 2004).

Placing so much emphasis on mannerly behavior and diplomatic skill is especially inappropriate in this case. It creates the impression that historical dynamism resides with elite actors and makes it more difficult to appreciate the extraordinary role of nonelite actors, such as Fannie Lou Hamer. In this way, the bias of traditional civil rights history obscures the complexity of the African American community along the lines of class and gender.

Significance of Findings

By drawing primary attention to the concept of black feminist consciousness, this book has made several important contributions to the field of political science. First and foremost, it has advanced the study of black women and politics by constructing a measure of black feminist consciousness. Second, it has overcome the deficiencies and limitations of existing research by focusing on the simultaneous effects of race and gender. Third, it has systematically investigated the impact of black feminist consciousness on overall political behavior in addition to various modes of political engagement. By so doing, the present study underscores the importance of studying gender differences in black public opinion and political behavior.

It is the case that few political scientists have written books and articles on the black female condition in the United States. Black female political scientists play a critical role in bringing to the academic fore the study of African American women and politics. Jewel Prestage, a political science professor at Prairie View A&M University, was the first African American woman to receive a doctorate in political science. She has opened up spaces for and directed critical attention toward the study of African American women in political science via empirical analysis of black female legislators. Still, much of the scholarship remains qualitative and is published in marginalized journals. That is to say, black feminist scholarship has not yet made a significant impact on the discipline of political science, and the academic work that has been done is hardly noted in the top journals. If we step back from an overview of the work cited here, we realize the fundamental importance of the project at hand.

Just as Nannie Helen Burroughs posed a challenge to the National Baptist Convention, I pose a similar challenge to the American Political Science Association and scholars of the profession who attempt to study specific strands of group consciousness without careful attention paid to other race-sex groups. I chose the title *Black Feminist Voices in Politics* because this book adds to the debate about a fundamentally flawed approach to the study of group consciousness whereby political scientists—black and white—willfully ignore multiple group identity and dichotomize black women's lives. Left unheard are black feminist voices in politics, which are ultimately rendered invisible in the scholarship on race and gender consciousness. To compel public opinion scholars and survey researchers to reconsider the ways in which they measure race and gender consciousness as separate, distinct categories is certainly no easy task when African American women are subjected to multiple burdens—for example, joblessness and domestic violence, teen pregnancy and illiteracy, poverty and malnutrition—that define their cumulative experience with race and gender oppression in the United States (Orfield and Ashkinaze 1991; Crenshaw 1993, 1995). Each debilitating problem cannot be treated as separate when the struggle to overcome one is engulfed by others. Thus, the biggest challenge facing empirical researchers is the problem of model misspecification when large national surveys often fail to include relevant variables for black people in general and black women in particular.

Overall, this research offers tantalizing evidence that black men and women report similar levels of black feminist consciousness. My definition of black feminist consciousness emphasizes its roots in the *recognition* of the double disadvantage faced by black women. From a theoretical perspective, both men and women can have black feminist consciousness. My empirical results support this understanding of black feminist consciousness. This is not an uncontroversial claim however, and I expect my findings will stimulate additional research on the topic at hand.

EPILOGUE
Stability and Change in
Attitudes toward Black Feminism

One thing about African American public opinion is clear. Both the women's liberation and the civil rights movements have had a profound effect on attitudes toward gender equality and feminist priorities among African Americans. It is not so much the case that black civil society has come to embrace feminisms, nor has it come to identify with the goals and objectives of the women's liberation movement per se. Rather, the effect is seen in the controversy that black feminism has engendered within African American communities concerning the simultaneity of oppression and the belief that such codependent variables as race, class, gender, and sexuality cannot be separated (or ranked) in lived experience. Given that the formation of African American public opinion takes place constantly as individual members of the race react to the world around them, it is likely that African American men and women reach full actualization of black feminist consciousness via day-to-day encounters with race, class, and gender oppression on the street, in the supermarket, and in other public spheres. African Americans are bombarded with persuasive communications daily, from media outlets and information networks, local black leaders and civil rights activists, and voluntary organizations and religious spaces to friends and family (Harris-Lacewell 2004). This flood of incoming information has a tremendous impact on the way African American men and women think about the simultaneity of oppression, which makes it especially difficult to predict the nature of African American public opinion and how it changes.

While the aggregate patterns and trends in race and gender (or feminist) consciousness have received considerable attention, relatively little is known about the level of support for black feminist consciousness over long periods of time. In light of this, I look to the past as well as the present to discover a "gender gap" in black feminist attitudes. Utilizing data from the 1993–1994 National Black Politics Study (NBPS) and the 2004–2005 National Black Feminist Study (NBFS), I update findings published in earlier work on attitudes toward black feminism among African Americans (Simien 2004; Simien and Clawson 2004). More specifically, I examine whether male and female respondents display a different level of support for black feminism than they did a decade ago. Along the way, I discover an important trend in African American public opinion that clearly attests to the fact that certain political attitudes are more persistent and consequential than others. For instance, I observe a gender gap in black feminist attitudes that points to a process whereby men are, in some cases, more likely to support black feminist tenets than are women. The male–female difference is attributable to an attitudinal shift on the part of men that persists over time. This finding is consistent with evidence reported in prior work, which suggested that a gender gap in African American public opinion toward gender equality and feminist priorities might become more pronounced in the future (Simien 2004). Item analysis reveals both the distinctiveness and the heterogeneity of African American public opinion. The attitudes of African American men are, on the whole, more liberal and progressive than the attitudes of African American women toward black feminist tenets. I also consider whether black feminist consciousness affects various modes of political behavior—for example, voting in presidential elections, contacting public officials and signing petitions, attending protest meetings or demonstrations, giving someone a ride to the polls, aiding a voter registration drive, and donating money to a campaign. I find that black feminist thinkers have been successful at disseminating their beliefs about the matrix of domination and galvanizing a mass following that actively participates in politics. I therefore conclude that black feminists have had a recognizable impact on the constituency they aim to serve.

Present Research

Given the findings reported in prior chapters, I anticipate a growing divide or gender gap in attitudes toward black feminism
among African Americans. While I understand that those results
are neither absolute nor fixed in time, my expectation is that the
male–female differential will *not* be attributable to any attitudinal
shift on the part of African American women but rather to growing liberalism on the part of African American men. Using data
from the 1993–1994 NBPS and the 2004–2005 NBFS, I extend
this work by determining the level of support for black feminist
consciousness in recent years and investigating whether black feminist consciousness stimulates active participation in politics. Until
recently, black feminist consciousness had not been formally defined and measured, let alone incorporated in empirical investigations of black political behavior (notable exceptions being Dawson
2001; Simien 2004; Simien and Clawson 2004). The present analysis of survey data allows me to investigate the extent to which
black feminist thinkers have been successful at disseminating their
core beliefs and galvanizing a mass following of African American
men and women who actively participate in politics.

Since the mid-1970s, black feminists have signed petitions,
staged mass rallies and protest demonstrations, testified before the
court of public opinion, and hosted educational workshops on college campuses. Despite this, however, the question that remains
unanswered is whether black feminist thinkers can realistically
compete in the ideological marketplace amid nationalist and liberal formations. Assuming that black feminist thinkers wish to
translate their ideas to mass political behavior, they must make
their intellectual pursuits available to nonelite actors. Ideally, black
feminist thinkers must merge theory and practice so as to impact
the lives of those most vulnerable to oppression. Otherwise, the
study of black feminist thought and praxis will remain largely limited with little prescriptive utility for individuals and groups that
confront interlocking systems of oppression.

At the heart of this epilogue are answers to two key questions:
Have black feminist thinkers made their intellectual work accessible
to those outside of academe—specifically, ordinary African American men and women? Does black feminist theorizing translate to

political behavior? In an effort to address these questions, I have two goals in mind. First, I determine the level of support for black feminist consciousness, and second, I assess the impact of black feminist consciousness on political behavior.

Data

The present study requires that attitudes toward black feminism among African Americans be measured on two separate occasions. To assess continuity and change in these attitudes, I compare two distinct samples of the adult African American population. The 1993–1994 NBPS is a unique study in that it contains questions that measure black feminist consciousness with multiple survey items at the core of black feminist thought. It was conducted between December 1993 and February 1994. The data for the NBPS was obtained from a national probability sample of all black households: 1,206 telephone interviews were completed, each one with an African American respondent who was eligible to vote. Modeled after the NBPS, the data for the 2004–2005 NBFS was obtained from a national probability sample of all black households: 500 telephone interviews were completed, each one lasting about fifteen minutes. To be eligible, respondents had to be both African American and eligible to vote. The survey was conducted between November 2004 and January 2005. It was administered by the Center for Survey Research at the University of Connecticut. Like the NBPS, the NBFS provides general information about the public attitudes and political preferences of voting-eligible African Americans. However, the primary focus of the NBFS centered on black feminist consciousness and its effect on various modes of political behavior. To facilitate comparisons, the survey includes several of the questions that measure black feminist consciousness derived from the 1993–1994 NBPS (Dawson, Brown, and Jackson 1993). Demographic information on respondents included sex, age, education, marital status, income, and employment status.

The Samples

Table 1 compares several important demographic characteristics between the NBFS and the NBPS. Looking at each sample separately,

Table 1
Characteristics of the Samples,
2004–2005 NBFS v. 1993–1994 NBPS

2004–2005 NBFS		1993–1994 NBPS	
Percent	N=500	Percent	N=1206
79	High School Graduate	83	High School Graduate
	Income		*Income*
11	Less than $10,000	12	Less than $10,000
15	$11,000–$20,000	22	$11,000–$20,000
11	$21,000–$30,000	20	$21,000–$30,000
26	$31,000–$50,000	23	$31,000–$50,000
22	More than $50,000	15	More than $50,000
15	DK/Refused	8	DK/Refused
	Marital Status		*Martial Status*
37	Married	36	Married
63	Not Married	64	Not Married
	Sex		*Sex*
44	Male	35	Male
56	Female	65	Female
	Age		*Age*
16	18–24	13	18–24
20	25–34	23	25–34
29	35–49	33	35–49
21	50–64	20	50–64
11	65 and over	11	65 and over
3	DK/Refused	0	DK/Refused
61	Employed	64	Employed

Source: 2004–2005 National Black Feminist Study (NBFS) and 1993–1994 National Black Politics Study (NBPS).

one of the most noticeable features is their remarkable degree of similarity. The sample's proximity to the NBPS statistics is important for drawing inferences to African Americans generally. As is often the case with telephone surveys of the adult African American population, a larger percentage of the sample is composed of women. However, the figure of 56 percent in the NBFS is better than that found in the NBPS. As usual in telephone surveys of African Americans that correlate census tract density information with directory-listed telephone households using a computer-assisted telephone interviewing system, the sample population is relatively older (Dawson 2001). The mean age for respondents ranged from thirty-seven for the NBFS and forty-three for the NBPS. They are also biased upwardly in terms of socioeconomic status in that high school dropouts make up 21 and 17 percent, respectively. In addition, one sample is slightly better at picking up the high end of the income distribution and the other the low end. Of course, this might be attributable to inflation.

Operational Definitions and Measures

Measurement items chosen for black feminist consciousness and political behavior have been examined previously (see chapters 3 and 5). Items used to measure black feminist consciousness have been tested at least once over the course of two surveys: the landmark 1993–1994 NBPS and the 2004–2005 NBFS. Items used to measure political behavior have been tested and retested over the course of several surveys: the landmark NES and the NBES. Comprised of those questions that best measure black feminist consciousness and political behavior, this research replicates operational definitions that typically set the standard. For this reason, it is not necessary to discuss them in detail here. See Appendix D for question wording and response choices.

Results and Analysis

The first goal was to determine who supports black feminist tenets. More specifically, I assess whether the level of support for black feminist consciousness differs across gender. Cross-tabulation was the method of choice, which helped organize, describe, and summarize observations. In this instance, the proportion of black women who possess black feminist consciousness was compared to the proportion of black men who support its fundamental tenets. Tables 2 and 3 present the results from the 2004–2005 NBFS and the 1993–1994 NBPS, respectively. The data show that black feminist attitudes did change somewhat; however, I recognize some striking stability that does not look fundamentally different from past patterns. It appears that black feminist intellectuals have been successful at disseminating their beliefs about the matrix of domination.

Table 2
Support for Black Feminist Consciousness in 2004–2005

	Black Women N=222	Black Men N=278	TOTAL N=500
The problems of racism, poverty, and sexual discrimination are all linked together. (ADDRESS ALL DISCRIMINATION)	67%**	79%**	72%
Black feminist groups help the black community by advancing the position of black women. (FEMINIST HELP COMMUNITY)	63%**	74%**	68%
Black women should share equally in the political leadership of the black community. (BLACK WOMEN LEADERSHIP)	95%	96%	96%
Black churches or places of worship should allow more women to become members of the clergy. (MORE WOMEN CLERGY)			
Agree	63%*	72%*	67%
Strongly Agree	47%	49%	48%
What generally happens to black women in this country will have something to do with your life. (LINKED FATE WITH BLACK WOMEN)	74%	75%	75%
Black women have suffered from both sexism within the black movement and racism within the women's movement. (BOTH MOVEMENTS)	75%	72%	74%

Source: 2004–2005 National Black Feminist Study.

Note: For the all of the items, except for the linked fate item, table entries are the percentage of respondents who indicated that they strongly agreed or somewhat agreed with that statement. For the linked fate item, the table entry is the percentage of respondents who indicated that they thought what generally happens to black women will affect them a lot or some.

*p ≤ .05; **p ≤ .01; for 2-tailed test.

Table 3

Support for Black Feminist Consciousness in 1993–1994

	Black Women N=781	Black Men N=425	TOTAL N=1,206
The problems of racism, poverty, and sexual discrimination are all linked together. (ADDRESS ALL DISCRIMINATION)	71%	68%	70%
Black feminist groups help the black community by advancing the position of black women. (FEMINIST HELP COMMUNITY)	69%	65%	68%
Black women should share equally in the political leadership of the black community. (BLACK WOMEN LEADERSHIP)	77%	79%	78%
Black churches or places of worship should allow more women to become members of the clergy. (MORE WOMEN CLERGY)			
Agree	54%	59%	55%
Strongly Agree	41**	53**	47%
What generally happens to black women in this country will have something to do with your life. (LINKED FATE WITH BLACK WOMEN)	70%	72%	71%
Black women have suffered from both sexism within the black movement and racism within the women's movement. (BOTH MOVEMENTS)	55%	49%	53%

Source: 1993–1994 National Black Politics Study.

Note: For the "more women clergy" item, the first table entry is the percentage of respondents who indicated that they strongly agreed or somewhat agreed with that statement and the second table entry is the percentage of respondents who indicated that they strongly agreed with that statement. For the "linked fate" item, the table entry is the percentage of respondents who indicated that they thought what generally happens to black women will affect them a lot or some.

*p < .05; **p < .01; for 2-tailed test.

Analysis of the 2004–2005 NBFS shows that roughly 72 percent of all respondents believe that racism, poverty, and sexual discrimination are linked together. Another 68 percent report that black feminist groups are beneficial to the black community. An even greater proportion endorse the notion that black women should share equally in the political leadership of the black community and express that what generally happens to black women in this country will have something to do with their own life— 96 percent and 75 percent, respectively. While there is less support for black female clergy, the majority 67 percent indicates that more black women should be allowed to become members of the clergy. These numbers reflect an upward trend in the level of support for black feminist consciousness for both sexes.

Analysis of the 1993–1994 NBPS showed that 70 percent of all respondents believed that racism, poverty, and sexual discrimination were linked together. Another 68 percent reported that black feminist groups were beneficial to the black community because they advance the position of black women. An even greater proportion, 78 percent, endorsed the notion that black women should share equally in the political leadership of the black community and 71 percent agreed that what generally happens to black women in this country will have something to do with their own life. While there was less support for black female clergy, the majority, 55 percent, indicated that more black women should be allowed to become members of the clergy.

The results from the 2004–2005 NBFS bore a striking resemblance to prior analysis of the 1993–1994 NBPS in that black feminist consciousness appears to be widespread for both sexes when African American women and men are studied together. The gender gap in African American public opinion becomes apparent when we examine African American men and women separately. When we examine those who agree that problems of racism, poverty, and sexual discrimination are linked together, a twelve-point difference exists between African American women and men. While an eleven-point difference exists when we examine those who agree with the statement that black feminist groups help the black community, a nine-point difference exists when we examine those who agree with the statement that black churches or places of worship should allow more women to become members of the clergy.

The fact that African American men are equally and, in some cases, more likely than African American women to support black feminist tenets in 2004–2005 clearly supports the findings that appear in prior research. Based on data from the 1984–1988 NBES and the 1993–1994 NBPS, I (Simien 2004) reported a similar trend in black attitudes toward gender equality and feminist priorities. Male–female differences reach statistical significance and thus cannot be dismissed in 2004–2005.

To date, scholars have debated the societal effects of such interrelated patterns as increased female participation in the paid labor force, better educational opportunities for women, the breakdown of the traditional family unit, and the transformation of gender roles in the home (Klein 1984). Perhaps the rise of single-parent, female-headed households in African American families might explain the gender gap in attitudes toward black feminism. Of course, more work must be done to conclusively link the rising incidence of single-parent, female-headed households among other factors to liberal attitudes toward gender equality and feminist priorities. Unfortunately, no survey items were available in either the 1993–1994 NBPS or the 2004–2005 NBFS to make this determination.

The second goal was to determine the effect of black feminist consciousness on political behavior. Table 4 presents the estimates for the regression model of political behavior separately for black women and men. The first important finding is that black feminist consciousness stimulates political behavior among black women. Both educational attainment and church attendance have a positive effect on black female political behavior. Marital status was also a significant predictor of political behavior for black women, indicating that single women are more likely to participate in American political processes. Such variables as income, home ownership, age, and urban residence were not significant predictors for black women. Table 4 also presents the estimates for the regression model of political behavior for black men, and the findings here differ from those reported above. While black feminist consciousness stimulates black male political behavior, such predictors as marital status and church attendance do not. Especially striking is the fact that only two variables—black feminist consciousness and educational attainment—predict black male political behavior.

Table 4
Determinants of Black Political Behavior,
Estimated Separately for Gender

Independent Variables	Black Women	Black Men
GROUP CONSCIOUSNESS		
BLACK FEMINIST	.207 **	.226 **
	(.069)	(.079)
SOCIOECONOMIC STATUS		
EDUCATION	.326 **	.224 **
	(.088)	(.094)
INCOME	.017	.067
	(.054)	(.053)
OTHER PREDICTORS		
URBAN RESIDENCE	.081	.077
	(.043)	(.048)
AGE	.035	.101
	(.064)	(.071)
HOME OWNERSHIP	.010	.022
	(.032)	(.035)
MARITAL STATUS	−.071 *	−.049
	(.030)	(.034)
CHURCH ATTENDANCE	.026 **	.050
	(.040)	(.046)
CONSTANT	−.100	−.147
	(.079)	(.084)
ADJUSTED R^2	.169	.115

Source: 2004–2005 National Black Feminist Study.

Table entries are unstandarized ordinary least squares regression coefficients, followed by the associated standard error. *$p \leq .05$; **$p \leq .01$; for 2-tailed test.

Next, I determined the effect of black feminist consciousness on various modes of political behavior. Tables 5 and 6 present the estimates for the regression models of voting, indirect and direct contact behavior, and communal and campaign activity separately for African American women and men. With regard to voting in

Table 5
Determinants of Various Modes of Political Behavior,
Estimated Separately for Black Women

Independent Variables	Voting	Indirect	Direct	Communal	Campaign
GROUP CONSCIOUSNESS					
BLACK FEMINIST	.528 **	.491 **	.280 **	.042	.126
	(.123)	(.120)	(.118)	(.106)	(.081)
SOCIOECONOMIC STATUS					
EDUCATION	.419 **	.502 **	.608 **	−.222	.360 **
	(.156)	(.152)	(.149)	(.134)	(.103)
INCOME	−.087	.082	.025	.076	.031
	(.096)	(.094)	(.092)	(.082)	(.064)
OTHER PREDICTORS					
URBAN RESIDENCE	.104	.152 *	.145 *	.131 *	.008
	(.077)	(.075)	(.074)	(.066)	(.051)
AGE	.234 **	.043	.057	−.199 *	.115
	(.114)	(.111)	(.109)	(.098)	(.076)
HOME OWNERSHIP	.121 *	.010	−.001	.003	.018
	(.056)	(.055)	(.054)	(.048)	(.037)
MARITAL STATUS	−.175 **	−.071	−.106 *	−.152 **	−.024
	(.054)	(.053)	(.052)	(.047)	(.036)
CHURCH ATTENDANCE	.085	.003	.055	.015	.028
	(0.72)	(.070)	(.069)	(.062)	(.048)
CONSTANT	.088	−.214	−.270 *	.209	−.108
	(.140)	(.137)	(.134)	(.120)	(.093)
ADJUSTED R^2	.188	.158	.159	.072	.073

Source: 2004–2005 National Black Feminist Study.

Table entries are unstandardized ordinary least squares regression coefficients, followed by the associated standard error. *p ≤ .05; **p ≤ .01; for 2-tailed test.

presidential elections, black feminist consciousness was statistically significant for both sexes. Other standard predictors of presidential voting for women included age, education, home ownership, and marital status, whereas for men income, urban residence, and church attendance were significant predictors. Given that the core themes of black feminist consciousness emphasize the importance

Table 6
Determinants of Various Modes of Political Behavior, Estimated Separately for Black Men

Independent Variables	Voting	Indirect	Direct	Communal	Campaign
GROUP CONSCIOUSNESS					
BLACK FEMINIST	.321 *	.296	.145	.064	.294 **
	(.143)	(.156)	(.157)	(.129)	(.095)
SOCIOECONOMIC STATUS					
EDUCATION	.070	.419 *	.470 *	.357 *	−.005
	(.170)	(.185)	(.186)	(.153)	(.112)
INCOME	.284 **	.020	.013	.112	.091
	(.097)	(.105)	(.106)	(.087)	(.064)
OTHER PREDICTORS					
URBAN RESIDENCE	.185 *	.131	.215 *	.066	.006
	(.087)	(.095)	(.095)	(.079)	(.058)
AGE	.009	−.003	.141	.055	.147
	(.129)	(.141)	(.142)	(.117)	(.085)
HOME OWNERSHIP	.017	.058	.062	−.089	.036
	(.063)	(.069)	(.069)	(.057)	(.042)
MARITAL STATUS	−.019	−.096	.044	−.071	−.059
	(.061)	(.067)	(.067)	(.055)	(.040)
CHURCH ATTENDANCE	.198 *	−.075	.065	−.066	−.165 *
	(.084)	(.092)	(.092)	(.076)	(.071)
CONSTANT	.148	−.056	−.248	−.007	−.198 *
	(.153)	(.167)	(.167)	(.138)	(.101)
ADJUSTED R^2	.120	.064	.063	.080	.091

Source: 2004–2005 National Black Feminist Study.

Table entries are unstandardized ordinary least squares regression coefficients, followed by the associated standard error. *$p \leq .05$; **$p \leq .01$; for 2-tailed test.

of political activism, a particularly interesting finding is that black feminist consciousness does not predict communal behavior for either sex. However, it clearly serves as an impetus for indirect and direct contact behavior among black women—that is, signing a petition in support of something or someone running for elective office as well as contacting a public official or agency. It also serves as an impetus for campaign activity among black men—that is, donating money, helping in a voter registration drive, giving people a ride to the polls, attending fund-raisers, and handing out campaign material. In this analysis, communal behavior was limited to taking part in a neighborhood march and attending a protest meeting. Considering that communal behavior was defined by merely two political activities, it seems reasonable to assume that an expanded model of communal behavior inclusive of either nonpolitical or additional political activities might yield different results. I contend that black feminist consciousness and its effect on communal behavior warrant further investigation, especially when considering that other variables such as urban residence, age, and marital status constitute the driving force behind communal activity for black women. While younger, single black women living in urban areas were more likely to engage in neighborhood marches and attend protest rallies, highly educated black men were more likely to participate in such activities because educational attainment constitutes the single predictor of communal behavior for black men. All in all, the effects of black feminist consciousness and socioeconomic status along with other standard predictors, such as age, urban residence, marital status, home ownership, and church attendance, on various modes of political behavior often differed across gender.

Conclusion

For years, African American men and women have exhibited similar aggregate patterns and trends in policy preferences and political partisanship. In fact, the search for a black gender gap was considered futile when studies revealed no appreciable differences in African American public opinion toward a series of issues ranging from military spending to social welfare (see, for example, Welch and Sigelman 1989). Not surprisingly, scholars paid little attention to these seemingly inconsequential findings as they were not extensively reported and summarized in subsequent research. For this reason, I expect the findings cited here to stimulate additional scholarly work when the obvious question that emerges is, Why should a black gender gap surface in the last two decades? Future research must therefore consider the theoretical importance of contextual factors. More specifically, future empirical investigations should continue to focus on intragroup differences and pay attention to gender role socialization and generational effects. Such a focus on how messages of gender role socialization are transmitted from mother to daughter as well as from father to son and how such information influences the development of black feminist consciousness would likely result in better models of black feminist support and predict the conditions under which black feminists of both sexes might support collaborative efforts to end patriarchy. It is also important to bear in mind that changes in aggregate attitudes may be at least partially the result of intergenerational differences. Younger generations have very different life experiences and values from those of older generations. Unlike the previous generation who came of age during the 1960s and 1970s when attitudes toward traditional sex-roles were changing, those who came of age during the 1980s and 1990s were more likely to grow up in a single parent household. That is to say, scholars must clarify the theoretical bases for expecting black men to be more supportive of gender equality and feminist priorities than are black women by identifying several factors not investigated in prior research—specifically, gender role socialization and generational effects.

Notably, this research dispels the notion that African American men have not supported nor have had any engagement with black feminism. Updating prior analysis, I show that the male–female differential in African American public opinion is attributable to growing liberalism on the part of African American men toward gender equality and feminist priorities. I recognize some striking stability in African American public opinion that does not look fundamentally different from past patterns and cycles of change, which means the present study provides additional evidence to support the claim that African American men have truly progressed in their thinking about traditional gender roles and have supported black feminist tenets for longer than many realize. African American women are similarly supportive of black feminist tenets, but to a lesser extent than African American men.

While many African American women may be aware of the ways in which male privilege and white privilege operate to erase their lives and perspectives, some African American men and women continue to hold the view that feminism is the cultural property of white women and that black women who identify with it are less authentically black. For this reason, African American women often feel that they must prioritize race over gender so as to avoid being labeled a traitor to the race (Simien and Clawson 2004). The dilemma of having to choose between race and gender constitutes a crisis for most African American women as they experience some sense of "internal conflict" when women's liberation is pitted against black civil rights.

Given that prior studies have neglected the importance of such intragroup relations in determining black public opinion and political behavior, additional research is necessary to examine this phenomenon in more detail. The present study represents a step forward in this regard, especially when considering black feminist consciousness is significantly related to black political behavior. Black citizens who recognize that the problems of racism, poverty, and sexual discrimination are linked together, that black feminists are beneficial to black communities, that black women should share equally in the political leadership and take on a more prominent role in the black church, and that they share a common fate with black women are more likely to actively participate in politics than those who do not subscribe to these core beliefs. To the extent that black politicians and civil rights activists value consensus issues over crosscutting issues, the study of the gender gap in attitudes toward black feminism and its over-time variation alerts us to issues relevant to gender that promote racial group consensus and, at the same time, stimulate various modes of political behavior.

All things considered, the importance of black women's leadership in pursuing egalitarian relations cannot be underemphasized or overstated when black patriarchy persists today. For example, black male rappers often affirm the dehumanization of African American women who are stereotyped as sexually promiscuous objects to be enjoyed and then discarded in their music videos. Thus, it has become necessary for black feminist intellectuals to establish an independent, organizational presence that extends beyond academic circles. That is to say, black feminist intellectuals must continue to exhibit the capacity for networking within and between marginalized groups by adhering to the norms of inclusive communicative democracy so as to engage those most vulnerable to oppression. Working in this way, black feminist intellectuals participate in a process of theorizing that speaks to concrete practice and lived experience. Then and only then will black feminists successfully mobilize the constituency they aim to serve: those outside of academe who have not had access to black feminist thought, who may have never heard the term used before, and who might come to recognize those circumstances that impinge upon the lives of black women—rape, domestic violence, sexual harassment, and sterilization abuse—are not divisive issues, but matters of vital concern to all people committed to social justice within and outside black communities. In this sense, black feminist theory has moral and ethical implications for how people live and relate to one another in this country.

APPENDIX A
Black Feminist Consciousness

All of the variables were coded on a 0 to 1 scale with 1 indicating greater support for black feminist consciousness.

"People have different ideas and opinions about politics. We would like to know what you think about the following matters. For the next several questions I'm going to give you two choices. Please tell us which choice is most true for you." (Some respondents volunteered "both"; those respondents were coded as a .5.)

> ADDRESS ALL DISCRIMINATION: The problems of racism, poverty, and sexual discrimination are all linked together and must be addressed by the black community, or blacks should emphasize the struggle around race.

> BLACK FEMINIST HELP COMMUNITY: Black feminist groups help the black community by working to advance the position of black women, or black feminist groups just divide the black community.

> BLACK WOMEN LEADERSHIP: Black women should share equally in the political leadership of the black community, or black women should not undermine black male leadership.

> COMMON FATE WITH BLACK WOMEN: Do you think that what generally happens to black women in this country will have something to do with what happens in your life? Will it affect you a lot, some, or not very much?

"I'm going to read some questions and please tell me if you strongly agree, somewhat agree, somewhat disagree, strongly disagree."

MORE WOMEN CLERGY: Black churches or places of worship should allow more women to become members of the clergy.

BOTH MOVEMENTS: Black women have suffered from both sexism within the black movement and racism within the women's movement, or black women mostly suffer from the same type of problems as black men.

APPENDIX B
Determinants of Black Feminist Consciousness

All of the variables were coded on a 0 to 1 scale with 1 indicating greater political engagement.

> RACE IDENTIFICATION: Do you think what happens generally to black people in this country will have something to do with what happens in your life? Will it affect you a lot, some, or not very much? (Respondents who indicated a lot were coded 1, and considered as having a high sense of race identification. Those who replied some were coded .66, those who responded not very much were coded .33, and respondents who said no were coded 0, and considered as having a low sense of race identification.)

> POWER DISCONTENT: On the whole, would you say that the economic position of blacks is better, about the same, or worse than whites? (Respondents who indicated that the economic position of blacks is better than whites were coded 0. Those who replied about the same were coded .5, and respondents who indicated worse than whites were coded 1.)

We are interested in how blacks are getting along economically. Would you say that blacks are getting along very well, fairly well, not too well, or not well at all? (Respondents who indicated blacks are getting along very well were coded 0. Those who indicated fairly well were coded .33, those who responded not too well were coded .66, and respondents who said not well at all were coded 1.)

MARITAL STATUS: Are you currently married, widowed, separated, divorced, have you never been married, or are you living with a significant other? (Respondents who responded married were coded 0, and all others were coded 1.)

EDUCATION: What is the highest grade of school or year of college you have completed? (Responses were coded in number of years completed along a 0 to 1 scale with 1 indicating the highest level of education completed.)

GENDER: Are you male or female? (Males were coded 0. Females were coded 1.)

EMPLOYMENT STATUS: In terms of your main activity are you working full time, working part time, temporarily laid off, unemployed, retired, homemaker, a student, or are you permanently disabled? (Respondents who responded working full time or part time were coded 1, all others were coded 0.)

URBAN RESIDENCE: Do you live in a rural or country area, a small town, a suburb of a city, or in a large city? (Respondents who indicated a large city were coded 1. Those who indicated a suburb were coded .75, those who responded a small city were coded .5, and those who responded small town were coded .25. Finally, respondents who indicated rural or country were coded 0.)

INCOME: Which of the following income groups includes your TOTAL FAMILY INCOME in 1992 before taxes? Up to $10,000; $10,000–$15,000; $15,000–$20,000; $20,000–$25,000; $25,000–$30,000; $30,000–$40,000; $40,000–$50,000; $50,000–$75,000; $75,000 and over. (The coding was from 0 [up to $10,000] to 1 [more than $75,000].)

RELIGIOSITY: How often do you attend religious services? Would you say at least once a week, once or twice a month, once or twice a year, or never? (Respondents who indicated never were coded 1. Those who responded once or twice a year were coded .66, and those who responded once or twice a month were coded .33. Finally, respondents who indicated once a week were coded 0.)

Aside from attending regular services, in the past twelve months have you been an active member of your church or place of worship? I mean, have you served on a committee, given time to a special project, or helped to organize a meeting? (Respondents who indicated yes were coded 0, and those who indicated no were coded 1.)

INTERVIEWER SEX: What is the interviewer sex? (Males were coded 0. Females were coded 1.)

AGE OF RESPONDENT: What was your age at your last birthday? (This item was coded as an eight-category variable: 0=0–19; .14=20–29; .29=30–39; .43=40–49; .57=50–59; .71=60–69; .86=70–79; 1=80+).

APPENDIX C
Race Consciousness

All of the variables were coded on a 0 to 1 scale with 1 indicating greater race consciousness.

GROUP IDENTIFICATION
COMMON FATE WITH BLACKS: Do you think what happens generally to black people in this country will have something to do with what happens in your life? [If yes] Will it affect you a lot, some, or not very much?

POWER DISCONTENT
"The next few questions deal with the economic conditions of your family, black Americans, and the nation."

BLACK ECONOMICS: We are interested in how blacks are getting along economically. Would you say that blacks are getting along very well, fairly well, not too well, or not well at all?

BLACK VS. WHITE ECONOMICS: On a whole, would you say that the economic position of blacks is better, about the same, or worse than whites? Is that much better or somewhat better? Is that much worse or somewhat worse?

SYSTEM BLAME

"Next we will ask a few questions which deal with your attitudes and opinions about racial change in America. Again, please tell me whether you strongly agree, somewhat agree, somewhat disagree, or strongly disagree."

UNFAIR OPPORTUNITY: American society has provided black people a fair opportunity to get ahead.

UNFAIR DEAL: American society just hasn't dealt fairly with black people.

"Please tell me which choice is most true for you."

SOCIETY UNFAIR: American society is fair to everyone OR American society is unfair to black people.

UNFAIR LEGAL SYSTEM: Generally, the American legal system treats all groups fairly OR the American legal system is unfair to blacks.

COLLECTIVE ACTION ORIENTATION

BLACK MOVEMENT: Do you think that the movement for black rights has affected you personally? [If yes] Did it affect you a lot, some, or not very much?

BLACK ORGANIZATION: Are you a member of any organization working to improve the status of black Americans? (Yes was coded 1, and no was coded 0.)

APPENDIX D
Political Behavior

All of the variables were coded on a 0 to 1 scale with 1 indicating greater political engagement.

"As I read from a list of political activities that people sometimes do, please tell me whether or not you have engaged in these activities in the last TWO years? Have you . . ." Respondents who replied yes were coded 1, and respondents who replied no were coded 0.

VOTING
PRESIDENTIAL: Did you vote in the past presidential election?

INDIRECT CONTACT BEHAVIOR
SIGNED PETITION SUPPORTING CANDIDATE: Signed a petition supporting a candidate who was running for office?

SIGNED PETITION SUPPORTING SOMETHING: Signed a petition in support of something or against something?

DIRECT CONTACT BEHAVIOR
CONTACTED PUBLIC OFFICIAL: Contacted a public official or agency?

CONTACTED BLACK ELECTED OFFICIAL: Ever contacted a BLACK elected official about a concern or problem that you have had?

165

CONTACTED WHITE ELECTED OFFICIAL: Ever contacted a WHITE elected official about a concern or problem that you have had?

COMMUNAL ACTIVITY

"Now, I'm going to read you a list of things people have done to address such problems as neighborhood crime, drug trafficking, the quality of education, or the safety of children. Please tell me if you have done any of these things in the last two years."

ATTEND PROTEST MEETING: Attended a protest meeting or demonstration?

TAKE PART IN MARCH: Taken part in a neighborhood march?

CAMPAIGN ACTIVITY

HELPED IN VOTER REGISTRATION: Helped in voter registration drive?

GIVE RIDE TO POLLS: Given people a ride to the polls on election day?

GIVE MONEY: Given money to a political candidate?

ATTEND FUND-RAISER: Attended a fund-raiser for a candidate?

HAND OUT CAMPAIGN MATERIAL: Handed out campaign material or placed campaign material on cars?

REFERENCES

Alexander-Floyd, Nikol G. 2003. "We Shall Have Our Manhood: Black Macho, Black Nationalism, and the Million Man March." *Meridians: Feminism, Race, and Transnationalism* 3(2): 171–203.

Andersen, Kristi, and Elizabeth Cook. 1985. "Women, Work, and Political Attitudes." *American Journal of Political Science* 29(2): 606–625.

Andrews, William L., ed. 2003. *Classic African American Women's Narratives*. New York: Oxford University Press.

Angus, Campbell, Philip E. Converse, Warren E. Miller, and Donald E. Stokes. 1960. *The American Voter*. New York: Wiley.

Ardrey, Saundra C. 1994. "The Political Behavior of Black Women: Contextual, Sructural, and Psychological Factors." In *Black Politics and Black Political Behavior: A Linkage Analysis*, ed. Hanes Walton Jr. New York: Praeger.

Baker, Phyllis, and Martha Copp. 1997. "Gender Matters Most: The Interaction of Gendered Expectations, Feminist Course Content, and Pregnancy in Student Course Evaluations." *Teaching Sociology* 25(1): 29–43.

Banaszak, Lee Ann, and Eric Plutzer. 1993a. "Contextual Determinants of Feminist Attitudes: National and Subnational Influences in Western Europe." *American Political Science Review* 87(1): 147–157.

———. 1993b. "The Social Bases of Feminism in European Community." *Public Opinion Quarterly* 57(1): 29–53.

Barker, Lucius, Mack Jones, and Katherine Tate. 1999. *African Americans and the American Political System*. Englewood Cliffs, NJ: Prentice Hall.

Barret, Edith. 1995. "The Policy Priorities of African American Women in State Legislatures." *Legislative Studies Quarterly* 22(2): 223–247.

———. 1997. "Gender and Race in the State House: The Legislative Experience." *Social Science Journal* 34(2): 131–144.

Baxter, Sandra, and Marjorie Lansing. 1981. *Women and Politics: The Visible Majority*. Ann Arbor: University of Michigan Press.

Beckwith, Karen. 1986. *American Women and Political Participation: The Impact of Work, Generation, and Feminism*. Westport, CT: Greenwood.

Benjamin, Lois. 1997. *Black Women in the Academy: Promises and Perils*. Gainesville: University Press of Florida.

Bernstein, Robert, Anita Chadha, and Robert Montjoy. 2001. "Overreporting Voting: Why It Happens and Why It Matters." *Public Opinion Quarterly* 65(1): 22–44.

Bogle, Donald. 1995. *Toms, Coons, Mulattoes, Mammies, and Bucks*. New York: Continuum.

Bohmer, Susanne, and Joyce L. Briggs. 1991. "Teaching Privileged Students About Gender, Race, and Class Oppression." *Teaching Sociology* 19(2): 154–163.

Bowen, William G., and Derek Bok. 1998. *The Shape of the River*. Princeton, NJ: Princeton University Press.

Brotz, Howard, ed. 1992. *African-American Social and Political Thought, 1850–1920*. New Brunswick, NJ: Transaction.

Browne, Irene, ed. 1999. *Latinas and African American Women at Work: Race, Gender, and Economic Inequality*. New York: Russell Sage Foundation.

Butler, Judith. 1988. "Performative Acts and Gender Constitution: An Essay in Phenomenology and Feminist Theory." *Theatre Journal* 40(4): 519–531.

Calhoun-Brown, Allison. 1999. "No Respect for Persons? Religion, Churches, and Gender Issues in the African American Community." *Women and Politics* 20(3): 27–43.

Carby, Hazel. 1997. "On the Threshold of the Woman's Era: Lynching, Empire, and Sexuality in Black Feminist Theory." In *Dangerous Liaisons,* ed. Anne McLintock, Aamir Mufti, and Ella Shohat. Minneapolis: University of Minnesota Press.

Carroll, Susan J. 1989. "The Personal is Political: The Intersection of Private Lives and Public Roles Among Women and Men in Elective and Appointive Office." *Women and Politics* 9(2): 51–68.

Clark, Cal, and Janet Clark. 1986. "Models of Gender and Political Participation in the United States." *Women and Politics* 6(1): 5–25.

Clawson, Rosalee A., and John A. Clark. 2003. "The Attitudinal Structure of African American Women Party Activists: The Impact of Race, Gender, and Religion." *Political Research Quarterly* 56(2): 211–221.

Cohen, Cathy. 1999. *The Boundaries of Blackness: AIDS and the Breakdown of Black Politics.* Chicago: University of Chicago Press.

Cohen, Cathy, Kathleen Jones, and Joan Tronto, eds. 1997. *Women Transforming Politics: An Alternative Reader.* New York: New York University Press.

Collier-Thomas, Bettye, and V. P. Franklin. 2001. *Sisters in the Struggle: African American Women in the Civil Rights–Black Power Movement.* New York: New York University Press.

Collins, Patricia Hill. 1990. *Black Feminist Thought.* 1st ed. New York: Routledge.

———. 1996. "What's in a Name? Womanism, Black Feminism, and Beyond." *Black Scholar* 26(1): 9–17.

———. 1998. *Fighting Words.* Minneapolis: University of Minnesota Press.

————. 2000. *Black Feminist Thought*. 2nd ed. New York: Routledge.

Conover, Pamela. 1988. "Feminists and the Gender Gap." *Journal of Politics* 50 (4): 985–1010.

Conway, Margaret. 1991. *Political Participation in the United States*. Washington, DC: CQ Press.

Cook, Elizabeth Adell. 1987. "Feminism and Group Consciousness in America." Ph.D. diss., Ohio State University.

————.1989. "Measuring Feminist Consciousness." *Women and Politics* 9(3): 71–88.

Cooper, Anna Julia. 1892. *A Voice from the South*. New York: Oxford University of Press.

————. 1995. "The Status of Woman in America." In *Words of Fire: An Anthology of African-American Feminist Thought,* ed. Beverly Guy-Sheftall. New York: New Press.

Crenshaw, Kimberle. 1993. "Demarginalizing the Intersection of Race and Sex: A Black Feminist Critique of Antidiscrimination Doctrine, Feminist Theory and Antiracist Politics." In *Feminist Legal Theory*, ed. D. Kelly Weisberg. Philadelphia: Temple University Press.

————. 1995. "Mapping the Margins: Intersectionality, Identity Politics, and Violence against Women of Color." In *Critical Race Theory,* ed. Kimberle Crenshaw et. al. New York: New Press.

Darcy, Robert, and Charles Hadley. 1988. "Black Women in Politics: The Puzzle of Success." *Social Science Quarterly* 69(3): 629–645.

Davis, Angela. 1981. *Women, Race, and Class*. New York: Vintage Books.

————. 1984. *Women, Culture, and Politics*. New York: Vintage Books.

Davis, Nancy J., and Robert V. Robinson. 1991. "Men's and Women's Consciousness of Gender Inequality: Austria, West

Germany, Great Britain, and the United States." *American Sociological Review* 56(1): 72–84.

Dawson, Michael C. 1994. *Behind the Mule: Race and Class in African-American Politics.* Princeton, NJ: Princeton University Press.

———. 1997. "African American Political Opinion: Volatility in the Reagan–Bush Era." In *African American Power and Politics,* ed. Hanes Walton Jr. New York, NY: Columbia University Press.

———. 2001. *Black Visions: The Roots of Contemporary African-American Political Ideologies.* Chicago: University of Chicago Press.

Dawson, Michael, Ronald Brown, and James Jackson. 1993. NATIONAL BLACK POLITICS STUDY Codebook (ICPSR 2018). Ann Arbor, MI : Inter-university Consortium for Political and Social Research.

Delgado, Richard, and Jean Stefancic, eds. 1997. *Critical White Studies.* Philadelphia: Temple University Press.

DuBois, Ellen Carol. 1978. *Feminism and Suffrage.* Ithaca, NY: Cornell University Press. DuBois, W. E. B. 1994. *The Souls of Black Folk.* New York: Dover.

Dugger, Karen. 1988. "Social Location and Gender-Role Attitudes: A Comparison of Black and White Women." *Gender and Society* 2(4): 425–448.

Evans, Sarah M. 1989. *Born for Liberty: A History of Women in America.* New York: Free Press.

Fischer, Frank. 1990. *Technocracy and the Politics of Expertise.* Newbury Park, CA: Sage.

Fogg-Davis, Hawley. 2003. "The Racial Retreat of Contemporary Political Theory." *Perspectives on Politics* 1(3): 555–564.

Foner, Philip S. ed. 1976. *Frederick Douglass on Women's Rights.* Westport, CT: Greenwood.

Fordham, Signithia. 1993. "Those Loud Black Girls: (Black) Women, Silence, and Gender Passing in the Academy." *Anthropology and Education Quarterly* 24(1): 3–32.

Fulenwider, Claire Knoche. 1980. *Feminism in American Politics.* New York: Praeger.

Gaines, Kevin K. 1996. *Uplifting the Race: Black Leadership, Politics, and Culture in the Twentieth Century.* Chapel Hill: University of North Carolina Press.

Gay, Claudine, and Katherine Tate. 1998. "Doubly Bound: The Impact of Gender and Race on the Politics of Black Women." *Political Psychology* 19(1): 169–184.

Giddings, Paula. 1984. *When and Where I Enter: The Impact of Black Women on Race and Sex in America.* New York: William Morrow.

Gilens, Martin. 1999. *Why Americans Hate Welfare.* Chicago: University of Chicago Press.

Gilkes, Cheryl Townsend. 2001. *If It Wasn't for the Women: Black Women's Experience and Womanist Culture in Church and Community.* Maryknoll, NY: Orbis Books.

Gooding-Williams, Robert. 1993. *Reading Rodney King, Urban Uprising.* New York: Routledge.

Gregory, Sheila T. 1999. *Black Women in the Academy.* New York: University Press of America.

Gurin, Patricia. 1985. "Women's Gender Consciousness." *Public Opinion Quarterly* 49(2): 143–163.

Gurin, Patricia, Shirley J. Hatchett, and James S. Jackson. 1989. *Hope and Independence.* New York: Russell Sage Foundation.

Guterbock, Thomas M., and Bruce London. 1983. "Race, Political Orientation, and Participation: An Empirical Test of Four Competing Theories." *American Sociological Review* 48(4): 439–453.

Guy-Sheftall, Beverly. 1995. *Words of Fire: An Anthology of African-American Feminist Thought.* New York: New Press.

Hancock, Ange-Marie. 2004. *The Politics of Disgust*. New York: New York University Press.

Harley, Sharon, and Rosalyn Terborg-Penn, eds. 1978. *The Afro-American Woman: Struggles and Images*. Port Washington, NY: Kennikat.

Harley, Sharon. 1996. "Nannie Helen Burroughs: The Black Goddess of Liberty" *Journal of Negro History* 81(1/4): 62–71.

Harley, Sharon, and Rosalyn Terborg-Penn, eds. 1978. *The Afro-American Woman: Struggles and Images*. Port Washington, NY: Kennikat.

Harmon-Martin, Shelia F. 1994. "Black Women in Politics: A Research Note." In *Black Politics and Black Political Behavior: A Linkage Analysis*, ed. Hanes Walton Jr. New York: Praeger.

Harris, Fredrick C. 1999. *Something Within: Religion in African American Political Activism*. New York: Oxford University Press.

Harris-Lacewell, Melissa. 2003. "The Heart of the Politics of Race: Centering Black People in the Study of White Racial Attitudes." *Journal of Black Studies* 34(2): 222–249.

———. 2004. *Barbershops, Bibles, and BET: Everyday Talk and Black Political Thought*. Princeton, NJ: Princeton University Press.

Hartman, Susan. 1989. *From Margin to Mainstream: American Women and Politics Since 1960*. New York: Knopf.

Henley, Nancy M., Karen Meng, Dolores O'Brien, William McCarthy, and Robert Sockloskie. 1998. "Developing a Scale to Measure the Diversity of Feminist Attitudes." *Psychology of Women Quarterly* 22(3): 317–348.

Herring, Mary, Thomas B. Jankowski, and Ronald E. Brown. 1999. "Pro-Black Doesn't Mean Anti-White: The Structure of African American Group Identity." *Journal of Politics* 61(2): 363–386.

Higginbotham, Evelyn Brooks. 1993. *Righteous Discontent.* Boston: Harvard University Press.

Hine, Darlene Clark, ed. 1993. *Black Women in America: An Historical Encyclopedia.* Brooklyn, NY: Carlson.

Hine, Darlene Clark, and Kathleen Thompson. 1998. *A Shining Thread of Hope: The History of Black Women in America.* New York: Broadway Books.

hooks, bell. 1981. *Ain't I a Woman.* Boston: South End.

———. 1984. *Feminist Theory: From Margin to Center.* Boston: South End.

———. 1989. *Talking Back.* Boston: South End.

Huggins, Nathan Irvin. 1980. *Slave and Citizen: The Life of Frederick Douglass.* New York: HarperCollins.

James, Joy. 1997. *Transcending the Talented Tenth: Black Leaders and American Intellectuals.* New York: Routledge.

James, Stanlie M., and Abena P.A. Busia. 1993. *Theorizing Black Feminisms: The Visionary Pragmatism of Black Women.* New York: Routledge.

Jaynes, David, and Robin Williams. 1989. *A Common Destiny: Blacks and American Society.* Washington, DC: National Academy Press.

Jewell, K. Sue. 1993. *From Mammy to Miss America and Beyond: Cultural Images and the Shaping of U.S. Social Policy.* London: Routledge.

———. 1990. *Quest for Equality: The Life and Writings of Mary Eliza Church Terrell, 1863–1954.* Brooklyn, NY: Carlson.

Jones, Mack. 1977. "Responsibility of Black Political Scientists to the Black Community" In *Black Political Scientists and Black Survival,* ed. Shelby Lewis Smith. Detroit: Balamp.

Jones, Tamara. 2000. "Building Effective Black Feminist Organizations." *Souls* 2 (4): 55–60.

Jordan, Emma Coleman. 1997. "Race, Gender, and Social Class in the Thomas Sexual Harassment Hearings: The Hidden Fault Lines in Political Discourse." In *Critical Race Feminism,* ed. Adrien Katherine Wing. New York: New York University Press.

Junn, Jane. 1997. "Assimilating or Coloring Participation? Gender, Race, and Democratic Political Participation." In *Women Transforming Politics,* ed. Cathy Cohen, Kathleen Jones, and Joan Tronto. New York: New York University Press.

Kane, Emily W., and Laura J. Macaulay. 1993. "Interviewer Gender and Gender Attitudes." *Public Opinion Quarterly* 57(1): 1–28.

Kelley, Robin. 1994. *Race Rebels: Culture, Politics, and the Black Working Class.* New York: Free Press.

King, Deborah. 1988. "Multiple Jeopardy, Multiple Consciousness: The Context of Black Feminist Ideology." *Signs* 14(1): 42–72.

King, Mae. 1975. "Oppression and Power: The Unique Status of Black Women in the American Political System." *Social Science Quarterly* 56(1): 117–128.

Klein, Ethel. 1984. *Gender Politics: From Consciousness to Mass Politics.* Cambridge, MA: Harvard University Press.

———. 1987. "The Diffusion of Consciousness in the United States and Western Europe." In *The Movements of the United States and Western Europe,* ed. Mary Fainsod Katzenstein and Carol McClurg Mueller. Philadelphia: Temple University Press.

Lee, Chana Kai. 1999. *For Freedom's Sake: The Life of Fannie Lou Hamer.* Urbana: University of Illinois Press.

Leighley, Jan E. 1990. "Social Interaction and Contextual Influences on Political Participation." *American Politics Quarterly* 18: 459–475.

———. 1995. "Attitudes, Opportunities, and Incentives: A Field Essay on Political Participation." *Political Research Quarterly* 48(1): 181–209.

Leighley, Jan E., and Arnold Vedlitz. 1999. "Race, Ethnicity, and Political Participation: Competing Models and Contrasting Explanations." *Journal of Politics* 61(9): 1092–1114.

Lein, Pei-te. 1998. "Does the Gender Gap in Political Attitudes and Behavior Vary Across Racial Groups?" *Political Research Quarterly* 51(4): 869–894.

Lerner, Gerda, ed. 1972. *Black Women in America: A Documentary History.* New York: Vintage.

Ling, Peter J., and Sharon Monteith, eds. 2004. *Gender and the Civil Rights Movement.* New Brunswick, NJ: Rutgers University Press.

Lorde, Audre. 1984. *Sister Outsider.* Freedom, CA: Crossing.

Loewenberg, James, and Ruth Bogin, eds. 1976. *Black Women in Nineteenth-Century American Life: Their Words, Their Thoughts, Their Feelings.* University Park: Pennsylvania State University Press.

Malveaux, Julianne. 1990. "Gender Differences and Beyond: An Economic Perspective on Diversity and Commonality among Women." In *Theoretical Perspectives on Sexual Difference,* ed. Deborah L. Rhode. New Haven, CT: Yale University Press

Mangum, Maurice. 2003. "Psychological Involvement and Black Voter Turnout." *Political Research Quarterly* 56(1): 41–48.

Mansbridge, Jane, and Katherine Tate. 1992. "Race Trumps Gender: Black Opinion on the Thomas Nomination." *PS* 25(3): 488–492.

Mattis, Jacqueline S. 2001. "Religion and African American Political Life." *Political Psychology* 22(2): 263–278.

McClain, Paula. 1996. "Black Politics at the Crossroads? Or in the Cross-Hairs?" *American Political Science Review* 90(4): 1211–1240.

McCombs, Harriet G. 1989. "The Dynamics and Impact of Affirmative Action Processes on Higher Education, the Curriculum, and Black Women." *Sex Roles* 21(1/2): 127–144.

Miller, Arthur H., Patricia Gurin, Gerald Gurin, and Oksana Malanchuk. 1981. "Group Consciousness and Political Participation." *American Journal of Political Science* 25(3): 494–511.

Mills, Kay. 1994. *This Little Light of Mine: The Life of Fannie Lou Hamer.* New York: Plume.

Moore, Valerie. 1996. "Inappropriate Challenges to Professorial Authority." *Teaching Sociology* 24(2): 202–206.

Moynihan, Daniel Patrick. 1965. *The Negro Family: The Case for National Action.* Washington, DC: U.S. Government Printing Office.

Mullane, Deirdre. 1993. *Crossing the Danger Water.* New York: Doubleday.

Naples, Nancy. 1998. *Grassroots Warriors: Activist Mothering, Community Work, and the War on Poverty.* New York: Routledge.

Neubeck, Kenneth, and Noel Cazenave. 2001. *Welfare Racism.* New York: Routledge.

Olsen, Marvin E. 1970. "Social and Political Participation of Blacks." *American Sociological Review* 35(4): 682–697.

Olson, Lynne. 2001. *Freedom's Daughters: The Unsung Heroines of the Civil Rights Movement from 1830 to 1970.* New York: Simon & Schuster.

Orfield, Gary, and Carole Ashkinaze. 1991. *The Closing Door: Conservative Policy and Black Opportunity.* Chicago: University of Chicago Press.

Painter, Nell Irvin. 1996. *Sojourner Truth: A Life, A Symbol.* New York: Norton and Company.

Payne, Charles M. 1995. *I've Got the Light of Freedom: The Organizing Tradition and the Mississippi Freedom Struggle.* Berkeley and Los Angeles: University of California Press.

Pierce, John C., William P. Avery, and Addison Carey Jr. 1973. "Sex Differences in Black Political Beliefs and Behavior." *American Journal of Political Science* 17(2): 422–430.

Prestage, Jewel. 1991. "In Quest of African American Political Woman." *Annals of the American Academy of the Political and Social Sciences* 515: 88–103.

Ransby, Barbara. 2000. "Black Feminism at Twenty-One: Reflections on the Evolution of a National Community." *Signs* 25(41): 1215–1221.

———. 2003. *Ella Baker and the Black Freedom Movement: A Radical Democratic Vision.* Chapel Hill: University of North Carolina Press.

Ransford, Edward, and Jon Miller. 1983. "Race, Sex, and Feminist Outlooks." *American Sociological Review* 48(1): 46–59.

Richardson, Marilyn, ed. 1987. Introduction to *Maria W. Stewart: America's First Black Political Writer.* Bloomington: Indiana University Press.

Roberts, Dorothy. 1997. *Killing the Black Body.* New York: Vintage Press.

———. 2002. *Shattered Bonds: The Color of Child Welfare.* New York: Basic Books.

Robinson, Deborah. 1987. "The Effect of Multiple Group Identity on Race Consciousness." Ph.D. diss, University of Michigan.

Robnett, Belinda. 1997. *How Long? How Long?: African American Women in the Struggle for Civil Rights.* New York: Oxford University Press.

Romero, Lora. 1997. *Home Fronts: Domesticity and Its Critics in the Antebellum United States.* Durham, NC: Duke University Press.

Rosenstone, Steven J., and John Mark Hansen. 1993. *Mobilization, Participation, and Democracy in America.* New York: Macmillan.

Roth, Benita. 2004. *Separate Roads to Feminism.* Cambridge: Cambridge University Press.

Rothenberg, Paula S. 1995. *Race, Class, and Gender in the United States: An Integrated Study.* New York: St. Martin's.

Rowe, Audrey, and John M. Jeffries. 1996. *The State of Black America.* New York: National Urban League.

Sapiro, Virginia. 2002. "It's the Context, Situation, and Question, Stupid: The Gender Basis of Public Opinion." In *Understanding Public Opinion,* ed. Barbara Norrander and Clyde Wilcox. Washington, DC: CQ Press.

Schechter, Patricia A. 1997. "Unsettled Business: Ida B. Wells Against Lynching, or How Antilynching Got Its Gender." In *Under Sentence of Death,* ed. W. Fitzhugh Brundage. Chapel Hill: University of North Carolina Press.

Schlozman, Kay Lehman, Nancy Burns, and Sidney Verba. 1994. "Gender and the Pathways to Participation: The Role of Resources." *Journal of Politics* 55(4): 960–990.

Shanley, Mary Lyndon. 1988. *Women's Rights, Feminism, and Politics in the United States.* Washington, DC: American Political Science Association.

Shingles, Richard D. 1981. "Black Consciousness and Political Participation: The Missing Link." *American Political Science Review* 75(1): 76–91.

Sidel, Ruth. 1996. *Keeping Women and Children Last.* New York: Penguin Books.

Simien, Evelyn M. 2001. "Black Feminist Consciousness: An Empirical Analysis of the Simultaneous Effects of Race and Gender on Political Behavior." Ph.D. diss., Purdue University.

———. 2003. "Black Leadership and Civil Rights: Transforming the Curriculum, Inspiring Student Activism." *PS: Political Science and Politics* 36(5): 747–750.

———. 2004. "Gender Differences in Attitudes Toward Black Feminism Among African Americans." *Political Science Quarterly* 119(2): 315–338.

————. 2005. "Race, Gender, and Linked Fate." *Journal of Black Studies* 35(5): 529–550.

Simien, Evelyn M., and Rosalee A. Clawson. 2004. "The Intersection of Race and Gender: An Examination of Black Feminist Consciousness." *Social Science Quarterly* 85(3): 793–810.

Smith, Barbara. 1995. "Some Home Truths about the Contemporary Feminists Movement." In *Words of Fire: An Anthology of African-American Feminist Thought,* ed. Beverly Guy-Sheftall. New York: New Press.

Smith, Jessie Carney, and Carrell P. Horton. 1997. *Statistical Record of Black America.* Detroit: Gale Research.

Smith, Robert C. 1996. *We Have No Leaders: African Americans in the Post–Civil Rights Era.* Albany: State University of New York Press.

Smooth, Wendy G., and Tamelyn Tucker. 1999. "Behind But Not Forgotten: Women and the Behind-the-Scenes Organizing of the Million Man March." In *Still Lifting, Still Climbing: African American Women's Contemporary Activism,* ed. Kimberly Springer. New York: New York University Press.

Spelman, Elizabeth V. 1988. *Inessential Woman: Problems of Exclusion in Feminist Thought.* Boston: Beacon.

Springer, Kimberly. 1999. *Still Lifting, Still Climbing: African American Women's Contemporary Activism.* New York: New York University Press.

Stanton, Elizabeth Cady, et al., eds. 1969. *History of Woman Suffrage.* New York: Source Book.

Staples, Robert. 1970. "The Myth of the Black Matriarchy." *Black Scholar* 1 (January–February): 8–16.

Sterling, Dorothy. 1979. *Black Foremothers: Three Lives.* Old Westbury, NY: Feminist Press.

————, ed. 1984. *We Are Your Sisters: Black Women in the Nineteenth Century.* New York: Norton.

Stone, Pauline Terrelonge. 1979. "Feminist Consciousness and Black Women." In *Women: A Feminist Perspective,* ed. Jo Freeman. Palo Alto, CA: Mayflower.

Sundquist, Eric J., ed. 1996. *The Oxford DuBois Reader.* New York: Oxford University Press.

Tate, Katherine. 1991. "Black Political Participation in the 1984 and 1988 Presidential Elections." *American Political Science Review* 85(4): 1159–1176.

———. 1994. *From Protest to Politics: The New Black Voters in American Elections.* Cambridge, MA: Harvard University Press.

Taylor, Shelley E. 1981. "A Categorization Approach to Stereotyping." In *Cognitive Processes in Stereotyping and Intergroup Behavior,* ed. David L. Hamilton. Hillsdale, NJ: Erlbaum.

Taylor, Ula. 1998. "The Historical Evolution of Black Feminist Theory and Praxis." *Journal of Black Studies* 29(2): 234–253.

Terborg-Penn, Rosalyn. 1998. *African American Women in the Struggle for the Vote, 1850–1920.* Bloomington: Indiana University Press.

Timpone, Richard. 1998. "Structure, Behavior, and Voter Turnout in the United States." *American Political Science Review* 92(1): 145–158.

Togeby, Lise. 1995. "Feminist Attitudes: Social Interests or Political Ideology." *Women and Politics* 15(4): 39–61.

Tonry, Michael. 1995. *Malign Neglect.* New York: Oxford University Press.

Turner, Caroline Sotello Viernes. 2002. "Women of Color in Academe." *Journal of Higher Education* 73(1): 74–93.

TuSmith, Bonnie, and Maureen T. Reddy. 2002. *Race in the College Classroom: Pedagogy and Politics.* New Brunswick, NJ: Rutgers University Press.

Vargas, Lucila. 1999. "When the 'Other' Is the Teacher: Implications of Teacher Diversity in Higher Education." *Urban Review* 31(4): 359–383.

———, ed. 2002. *Women Faculty of Color in the White Classroom*. New York: Peter Lang.

Verba, Sidney, Nancy Burns, and Kay Lehman Schlozman. 1997. "Knowing and Caring about Politics: Gender and Political Engagement." *Journal of Politics* 59(4): 1051–1072.

Verba, Sidney, and Norman H. Nie. 1972. *Participation in America: Political Equality and Social Equality*. Chicago: University of Chicago Press.

Verba, Sidney, Kay Lehman Schlozman, Henry Brady, and Norman Nie. 1993. "Who Participates? What Do They Say? *American Political Science Review* 87(2): 303–318.

———. 1995. *Voice and Equality: Civic Voluntarism in American Politics*. Cambridge, MA: Harvard University Press.

Walker, Alice. 1983. *In Search of Our Mother's Gardens*. New York: Harcourt Brace.

Washington, Mary Helen. 1988. Introduction to *A Voice from the South*, by Anna Julia Cooper. New York: Oxford University Press.

Waters, Kristin, ed. 2000. *Women and Men Political Theorists: Enlightened Conversations*. Malden, MA: Blackwell.

Weitz, Rose, and Leonard Gordon. 1993. "Images of Black Women Among Anglo College Students." *Sex Roles* 28(1/2): 19–34.

Welch, Susan, and Lee Sigelman. 1989. "A Black Gender Gap?" *Social Science Quarterly* 70(1): 120–133.

Welch, Susan. 1977. "Women as Political Animals? A Test of Some Explanations for Male–Female Differences." *American Journal of Political Science* 21(4): 711–730.

White, Deborah Gray. 1985. *Ar'n't I a Woman?: Female Slaves in the Plantation South*. New York: Norton.

———. 1999. *Too Heavy a Load: Black Women in Defense of Themselves, 1894–1994*.

White, John. 1985. *Black Leadership in America.* New York: Longman.

Wilcox, Clyde. 1990. "Black Women and Feminism." *Women and Politics* 10(3): 65–84.

———. 1991. "The Causes and Consequences of Feminist Consciousness among Western European Women." *Comparative Political Studies* 23(4): 519–545.

———. 1997. "Race and Gender Consciousness Among African American Women: Sources and Consequences." *Women and Politics* 17(1): 73–94.

Wilcox, Clyde, and Sue Thomas. 1992. "Religion and Feminist Attitudes Among African-American Women: A View from the Nation's Capitol." *Women and Politics* 12(2): 19–40.

Williams, Linda. 1987. "Black Political Progress in the 1980s: The Electoral Arena." In *The New Black Politics,* ed. Michael B. Preston, Lenneal J. Henderson, and Paul L. Puryear. New York: Longman.

Williams, Patricia J. 1991. *The Alchemy of Race and Rights.* Boston: Harvard University Press.

Williams, Sherley Anne. 1990. "Some Implications of Womanist Theory." In *Reading Black, Reading Feminist: A Critical Anthology,* ed. Henry Louis Gates Jr. New York: Meridian.

Wilson, William Julius. 1996. *When Work Disappears.* New York: Vintage.

———.1998. *The Bridge Over the Racial Divide.* Berkeley and Los Angeles: University of California Press.

Wing, Adrien Katherine, ed. 1997. *Critical Race Feminism.* New York: New York University Press.

Wolfinger, Raymond E., and Steven J. Rosenstone. 1980. *Who Votes?* New Haven, CT: Yale University Press.

Yee, Shirley J. 1992. *Black Women Abolitionists: A Study of Activism, 1828–1860.* Knoxville: University of Tennessee Press.

Young, Iris Marion. 1997. *Intersecting Voices*. Princeton, NJ: Princeton University Press.

———. 2000. *Inclusion and Democracy*. New York: Oxford University Press.

Zinn, Maxine Baca, and Bonnie Thornton Dill. 1996. "Theorizing Difference from Multiracial Feminism." *Feminist Studies* 22 (2): 321–331.

INDEX

Activism: black female, 1, 2, 10; civil
rights, 3; commitment to, 123;
feminist, 70; grassroots, 1, 2, 20,
96, 129, 134; integration in daily
living, 22; intellectual, 66, 87;
political, 11, 24, 65, 87, 89; trig-
gered by hardship, 66; unrecognized, 10
Affirmative action, 73, 74, 90; gen-
der/race identity and, 38
Africana womanism, 130, 131
Age: black feminist consciousness and,
16; as determinate of feminist
support, 70, 82, 83*tab*, 86*tab*;
political participation and, 99,
149*tab*, 150*tab*
Alexander-Floyd, Nikol, 11
American Association of University
Women, 116
American National Election Studies
(1972–1976), 59
American Political Science Association,
137
Analysis items and themes: ADDRESS
ALL DISCRIMINATION, 45,
47*tab*, 48, 53, 53*tab*, 54, 54*tab*,
55*tab*, 81, 103, 145*tab*, 146*tab*;
BLACK WOMEN LEADER-
SHIP, 46, 47*tab*, 53, 53*tab*, 54,
54*tab*, 55*tab*, 81, 103, 145*tab*,
146*tab*; BOTH MOVEMENTS,
45, 47*tab*, 48, 52, 53, 53*tab*, 54,
54*tab*, 55*tab*, 57, 58, 82, 103,

145*tab*, 146*tab*; COLLECTIVE
ACTION ORIENTATION, 103,
110*tab*; on determinates of feminist support, 144–152; FEMI-
NIST HELP COMMUNITY, 46,
47*tab*, 53, 53*tab*, 54, 54*tab*,
55*tab*, 81, 103, 145*tab*, 146*tab*;
gender equality in black community, 45, 46; of impact of black
feminist consciousness on political behavior, 144–152; of independent variables, 82–87;
intersectionality, 45; LINKED
FATE WITH BLACK WOMEN,
46, 47*tab*, 53, 53*tab*, 54, 54*tab*,
55*n*, 55*tab*, 82, 103, 145*n*,
145*tab*, 146*n*, 146*tab*; MORE
WOMEN CLERGY, 10, 11, 35,
46, 47*tab*, 53, 53*tab*, 54, 54*tab*,
55*n*, 55*tab*, 56, 81, 103, 145*tab*,
146*n*, 146*tab*; POWER DIS-
CONTENT, 104, 110*tab*; predictive factors, 47*tab*; predictive
validity and, 49; SYSTEM
BLAME, 103, 110*tab*; variables
defined, 157–158
Anderson, Kristi, 68
Andrews, William, 63, 66
Angus, Campbell, 97, 100
Anthony, Susan B., 3, 21, 42, 43
Antislavery movements, 2
Ardrey, Saundra, 128
Avery, William, 33

185

Awareness: acute sense of, 2, 8; racial, 33, 48

Baker, Phyllis, 74, 75
Banaszak, Lee Ann, 68, 69, 70
Barker, Lucius, 33
Barrett, Edith, 95
Baxter, Sandra, 33, 95, 128
Beckwith, Karen, 100, 101, 109
Behind the Mule: Race and Class in African-American Politics (Dawson), 28, 34
Benjamin, Lois, 74, 75
Bernstein, Robert, 107
Black Panther Party, 12
Black Visions (Dawson), 4
Bogle, Donald, 72
Bohmer, Susanne, 74
Boundaries of Blackness (Cohen), 31
Bowen, William, 73
Brady, Henry, 115
Brotz, Howard, 21
Brown, Ronald, 6, 7
Browne, Irene, 9, 76
Burroughs, Nannie Helen, 13, 119–121, 137
Busing: gender/race identity and, 38; political participation and, 113
Butler, Judith, 30

Calhoun-Brown, Allison, 98, 115
Carby, Hazel, 20, 21
Carey, Addison, 33
Carroll, Susan, 109
Catt, Carrie Chapman, 21
Church, black: gender equality and, 77, 78; importance as social institution, 56, 57; male domination in, 57, 77, 78; role in inhibiting development of feminist consciousness, 56, 61, 126; sexism in, 57, 77, 78; teaching of gender inequality in, 56, 57, 77, 78; validation of patriarchy by, 10, 35
Civil Rights Bill (1875), 19

Civil rights movement, 3, 10, 11, 64, 135, 139; black women's participation in, 32, 33; women shunned as representatives of, 112
Clark, Cal, 109
Clark, Janet, 109
Class: everyday experiences of, 11; exploitation, 9, 56, 84, 89; identity, 85; internal political efficacy and, 28; political orientation differences, 28
Classism, 10
Clawson, Rosalee, 28
Coalitions: with black men, 13; building of, 11, 13; multi-racial, 4, 129; women's, 122
Cohen, Cathy, 31, 95
Collier-Thomas, Bettye, 135
Collins, Patricia, 4, 8, 10, 11, 17, 25, 26, 32, 33, 39, 60, 64, 65, 70, 71, 72, 76, 112, 124
Community, black: assertions of black masculinity in, 12; benefits of feminism to, 11; black feminist consciousness and, 98; gender inequality in, 10; hierarchy of interests in, 5, 12, 27, 52, 58; political alliances and, 66; race prioritized over gender in, 12, 77
Conover, Pamela, 12, 22, 23, 26, 123, 124
Consciousness: double, 8, 29, 30, 31; effect of multiple group identity on, 37; feminist, 24–27; gender-related, 24–27, 98, 124; integration into daily living, 22; of race, 31; raising, 70, 96; structural/demographic determinants of, 68
Consciousness, black feminist, 24–27. *See also* Analysis items and themes; Feminism, black; age and, 16, 70, 82, 83*tab,* 86*tab,* 87; alternative approaches in, 133–136; benefit to black com-

munity of, 98, 122; changes in gender responses to over long term, 140–155; conceptualization of, 15, 21; concrete experiences and, 14; daily encounters with oppression and, 70; defining, 9–11; determinants of, 16, 63–91, 159–161; development of, 14; differing components across gender in, 41–62; dimensionality of, 16; distinct from race identification, 15, 41–62, 98; distinction from feminist consciousness, 46–60, 125; early manifestations of, 2; education and, 16, 68–69, 79, 83*tab*, 86*tab*, 87, 160; emphasis on simultaneous effects of race and gender in, 36–39; empirical assessments of, 12–13, 15; employment status and, 16, 69–70, 79, 83*tab*, 86*tab*, 160; feminist identity and, 41–62; full actualization of, 139; gender determinates of feminist support, 126; gender equality and, 98; gender gap in attitudes to, 15, 140–155; impact of on modes of black political participation, 96–118; income levels and, 16, 69, 79, 82, 83*tab*, 85, 86*tab*, 160; individual characteristics and, 14; inhibition of development by black church, 56, 61; intersecting patterns of discrimination in, 7; intersectionality and, 5, 98, 122; interviewer sex and, 16; lack of large enough sample in surveys, 24–27; level of support for, 13, 16, 41–62, 140; linked fate with other black women in, 98, 122; long-term support for, 140; marital status and, 16, 71–76, 83*tab*, 84, 86*tab*; measurement of, 6, 45–46, 125; objective conditions and, 14;

political participation and, 16, 96–118; power discontent and, 16, 71, 79, 83*tab*, 84, 86*tab*, 159; race identity and, 16, 52, 76–77, 79, 83*tab*, 86*tab*, 159; race loyalty and, 48; recognition of double disadvantage in, 137; religiosity and, 16, 77–78, 79, 83*tab*, 84, 86*tab*, 161; residential status and, 16, 70–71, 79, 83*tab*, 86*tab*, 160; sex of research interviewers and, 78, 79, 83*tab*, 85, 86*tab*, 161; shaping of political activities by, 1, 2; significance of research on, 67–68, 136–137; support for, 41–62, 145*tab*, 146*tab*; support from black men, 53, 54, 54*tab*; thermometer ratings and, 49, 50, 50*tab*, 52, 123; understanding, 1; variables affecting, 63–91

Consciousness, gender, 5; intersection with race, 5

Consciousness, group: absence of black feminist voices in, 14; black political behavior and, 96–118; collective action orientation and, 22, 98; as collective resource for African Americans, 22; commitment to group strategies and, 23; concealment of political orientations of African American women and, 23; cross-cutting *vs.* consensus issues in, 15, 31; defined in terms of race and gender, 7; determination of political behavior and, 22; differences from black feminism, 5; and disadvantaged status, 9; dominant conceptualization of, 8, 21, 22, 23; effect of dominant conceptualization of in politicized identification of black women, 15, 21; group identification in, 22; implications for

.

Consciousness, group (*continued*):
political behavior and, 39; ineffective conceptualizations of,
123; literature on, 22–23; measurement of, 5, 8; measurement
of race and gender consciousness
in, 23; perceived self-location in,
22; political behavior and, 15,
21, 27–29; political participation
and, 149*tab*, 150*tab*, 151*tab*;
power discontent and, 22, 98;
public opinion and, 23; race
identity and, 98; simultaneous effects of race and gender, 7; status
deprivation and, 22; structural
barriers and, 23; system blame
and, 22, 98; understanding, 1
Consciousness, race, 5, 76–77,
96–118, 163–164; collective
action and, 110*tab*; collective
action orientation and, 97, 102;
effect of multiple group identity
on, 36–39; group discontent and,
110*tab*; group identification and,
110*tab*; intersection with gender,
5; measurement of, 102; political
participation and, 96–118; power
discontent and, 97, 102; race
identity and, 97, 102; system
blame and, 97, 102, 110*tab*
Conservatism, black, 4
Conway, Margaret, 97, 100
Cook, Elizabeth, 12, 23, 68, 70, 123,
124
Cooper, Anna Julia, 1, 2, 3, 8, 13, 21,
65, 121
Crenshaw, Kimberle, 49, 56, 122, 137
Crummell, Alexander, 21

Darcy, Robert, 28
Davis, Angela, 8, 25, 42, 43, 56, 72,
76, 124
Dawson, Michael, 4, 5, 6, 9, 11, 20,
22, 23, 28, 34, 39, 56, 97, 122,
142, 144

Delaney, Martin, 21
Delgado, Richard, 74
Discrimination: affirmative action and,
73, 74; against African American
men, 32; blockbusting as, 87; in
employment, 120; gender, 9, 14,
89; intersecting patterns of, 37;
literacy tests, 87; past, 87; racial,
9, 11, 14, 32, 116; redlining as,
87; rejection of intellectual work
in, 8; reverse, 74; sex, 26, 48, 116;
status deprivation and, 9; steering
as, 87
Douglass, Frederick, 20, 21, 41, 42,
43, 56
DuBois, W.E.B., 2, 3, 8, 9, 21, 29, 30,
31
Dugger, Karen, 95

Education, 9; access to, 95–96; black
feminist consciousness and, 16;
as determinate of feminist support, 68–69, 79, 83*tab*, 86*tab*,
87; equal opportunities in, 120;
failure to meet needs of African
American women, 2; and gender
inequality, 68–69; gender/race
identity and, 38; industrial, 120;
liberal arts, 2; participatory resources from, 97; political participation and, 95, 99
Employment status, 9; black feminist
consciousness and, 16; compulsory, 76; as determinate of feminist support, 69–70, 79, 82,
83*tab*, 86*tab*; discrimination in,
120; gender equality and, 69;
labor market segregation and, 56,
71; political participation and,
95; sex disparities and, 70
Equal Rights Amendment, 24, 116
Equal Rights Association, 42
Evans, Sarah, 21
Experiences: complexity of black
female, 15; concrete, 14; cumula-

tive, 137; everyday, 11, 20, 39, 89, 94, 122, 139; factors of black feminist consciousness rooted in, 63–67; group loyalty and, 11; layered, 10; linked fate and, 34; lived, 2, 10, 14, 30, 34, 66, 67, 73, 139; shared, 11; totality of black female, 37; transformation of, 39; turned into resistance, 94; of white, middle-class women, 25

Feminism: Africana womanism and, 130, 131; assumptions on comparability of black/white, 12, 84, 122; as cultural property of white women, 32, 153; feeling thermometer ratings, 25, 26, 123; politics of, 68; priorities in, 12, 27; and race loyalty, 27; treatment of African American concerns as secondary in, 25; variables influencing, 67, 68; ways individuals come to adopt, 67; white, 25, 51; woman's centered perspective, 26
Feminism, black: adoption of, 16; benefit to community, 11; commitment to activism in, 123; competition in ideological marketplace and, 141; core ingredients of, 5; deficiencies in measurement of support for, 24, 25; desire of white feminists to build alliances with, 129; determinants of, 63–91; early, 3; experiences of black women and, 5; factors in adoption of, 14; focus on community-centered politics in, 5; gender attitudes on, 58, 59, 59tab, 60; gender differences in support for, 55tab, 56, 82–87, 140–155; gender equality and, 24, 25; ideology and, 39; intellectual inquiry into, 3; intellectual roots

of, 2; potential to overcome social difference, 4; priorities of, 4; from private to public sphere, 65–66; as social justice project, 11; stability/change in attitudes on, 139–155; support for, 14, 58, 59, 59tab, 60, 61; support for among men, 13; theory, 3, 7–9, 19–40; variables affecting perspectives of, 16; working outside mainstream feminist organizations, 24, 25
Fischer, Frank, 132
Fogg-Davis, Hawley, 4
Foner, Philip, 42, 43
Food stamps, 113; gender/race identity and, 38
Fordham, Signithia, 71
Fortune, T. Thomas, 21
From Protest to Politics:The New Black Voters in American Elections (Tate), 28, 32
Fulenwider, Claire, 25, 26, 59, 68, 69, 124

Gage, Frances Dana, 43
Gaines, Kevin, 2, 3
Gay, Claudine, 12, 13, 16, 23, 27, 28, 37, 38, 51, 52, 112, 115, 124
Gender: analysis of determinates of feminist support and, 82–87; attitudes toward equality, 148; class-based differences in attitudes toward equality, 130; consciousness, 5, 23, 24–27, 25, 98; defining, 32; discrimination, 9, 14, 89; equality, 4, 10, 12, 24, 25, 27, 125; gap, 33; identity, 12, 30, 36–39, 85, 123; inequality, 68; intersection with race, 36–39; liberal policy positions and, 38; linked fate and, 34; naturalization of, 30, 31; norms, 96; oppression, 8, 122, 137; political participation and, 99, 108, 108tab, 109, 111tab; prioritized

Gender (*continued*): over race, 77;
    privilege, 71; public opinion and,
    13; race prioritized over, 7, 44,
    49, 56, 57, 58; religiosity and,
    35; roles, 6, 26, 59, 74, 126;
    role stereotypes, 35; socializa-
    tion to, 40; subordination, 11;
    theorizing, 28, 29–36
Giddings, Paula, 2, 3, 10, 64
Gilens, Martin, 73
Gilkes, Cheryl, 120
Gooding-Williams, Robert, 56, 71
Gregory, Sheila, 74, 75
Gurin, Patricia, 22, 23, 97, 98, 102
Guterbock, Thomas, 100, 101
Guy-Sheftall, Beverley, 2, 3, 26, 32,
    48, 60, 64, 70, 76, 122, 124

Hamer, Fannie Lou, 135, 136
Harley, Sharon, 3, 120
Harmon-Martin, Shelia, 29, 128
Harper, Frances, 13, 41, 43
Harris, Fredrick, 10, 11, 28, 35, 56,
    57, 77, 98, 115
Harris-Lacewell, Melissa, 127, 139
Hatchett, Shirley, 7, 22
Henley, Nancy, 16, 68
Herring, Mary, 34
Heterosexism, 10, 11, 89
Higginbotham, Evelyn, 10, 57, 119,
    120
Hill, Anita, 11, 27, 67
Hine, Darlene, 19, 43, 64, 65, 120
History of Woman Suffrage, 40
Homes for Girls, 95
hooks, bell, 8, 10, 24, 25, 70, 71, 95,
    124
Hudson-Weems, Clenora, 130
Huggins, Nathan, 42

Identity: class, 85; constituted, 30; dual,
    8, 15; feminist, 26, 123; gender,
    30, 36–39, 77, 85, 123; group, 11,
    22; mapping, 31; multiple group,
    37, 76–77, 89, 137; perceived self-

location and, 22, 97; rac, 33; race,
    36–39, 76–77, 85, 123; sense of
    belonging and, 97
Illiteracy, 9
Income levels, 9; black feminist con-
    sciousness and, 16; as determi-
    nate of feminist support, 69, 79,
    82, 83*tab,* 85, 86*tab;* political
    participation and, 97, 99, 149*tab,*
    150*tab,* 151*tab*
"Interviewer Gender and Gender
    Attitudes" (Kane), 78

Jackson, James, 6, 7
James, Joy, 2, 3, 20, 21
James, Stanlie, 8, 91
Jaynes, David, 9, 56
Jewell, K. Sue, 8, 72, 76
Jones, B., 93, 116
Jones, Mack, 1, 17
Jones, Tamara, 10, 95, 122
Jordan, Emma, 27, 32, 73, 124
Junn, Jane, 33

Kane, Emily, 78
Kelley, Robin, 134
King, Deborah, 9, 26, 70, 76, 122, 124
King, Mae, 9, 26, 71, 124
Klein, Ethel, 22, 23, 24, 68, 69, 71,
    83, 148

Lansing, Marjorie, 33
Leadership, black: clerical, 35; effec-
    tiveness in post-civil rights era,
    90, 91; male domination of, 2,
    10, 11, 35; marginalization of
    black women by, 3
Lee, Chana Kai, 112
Leighley, Jan, 96, 97
Lein, Pei-te, 33, 95
Lerner, Gerda, 2
Liberation, black, 11, 64; assertion of
    black masculinity and, 20; hin-
    dering, 48; need to avoid diffu-
    sion of energy in, 48

Liberation, women's, 64, 68, 123, 124, 139
Ling, Peter, 135
Linked fate: gender and, 34; group identification and, 34; lived experiences and, 34
Loewenberg, James, 2
Lorde, Audre, 10, 124
Lynching, 19, 20

Malveaux, Julianne, 9
Mangum, Maurice, 128
Mansbridge, Jane, 24, 27
Marital status: black feminist consciousness and, 16; as determinate of feminist support, 71–76, 83tab, 84, 86tab; political participation and, 98, 99, 104, 111, 149tab, 150tab, 151tab
Marxism, black, 4
Mattis, Jacqueline, 134
McClain, Paula, 90
McCombs, Harriet, 74
"Measuring Feminist Consciousness" (Cook), 25, 123
Medicare spending, 113; gender/race identity and, 38
Men, African American: analysis of determinates of feminist support, 82–87; awareness of predicament of black women by, 9; benefits of patriarchy and, 71, 84; chauvinistic attitudes in, 64; criticism of authority of, 64; gender equality and, 4; identification with black women as marginalized, 56, 61; long-term attitudes toward black feminism, 140–155; notions of respectable manhood and, 2; political behavior determinants, 151tab; political orientations of, 28; protection from racism for, 7, 44, 49; subordinated to white men in occupational structure, 56; support for

feminist priorities, 4, 88, 125, 126; traditional gender roles and, 57
Miller, Arthur, 22, 97, 102
Million Man March, 10, 11, 27
Mills, Kay, 112
Mississippi Freedom Democratic Party, 112
Moore, Valerie, 74, 75
Mothers' Clubs, 95
Mott, Lucretia, 21
Movements: antislavery, 2; black power, 12; civil rights, 10, 11, 19, 21, 64, 139; nationalistic, 12; women's liberation, 3, 24, 64, 68; women's suffrage, 2
Moynihan, Daniel Patrick, 72
Muckraking, 20
Mullane, Deirdre, 19, 116

Naples, Nancy, 132, 133, 134
National Association for the Advancement of Colored People (NAACP), 95
National Association of Colored Women (NACW), 94, 95
National Association of University Women, 116
National Baptist Convention, 119, 120, 137; Women's Convention Auxiliary, 119, 120, 121
National Black Election Studies (1984–1988 and 1996), 6, 28, 62; data analysis from, 44–60; effects of multiple group identity on race consciousness, 37; gender measurements on, 126; simultaneous effects of gender and race on liberal policy in, 38, 39; support for feminist position on, 58, 59, 59tab, 60
National Black Feminist Organization, 129

National Black Feminist Study
(2004–2005): data on long-term
support for black feminism and,
140–155
National Black Politics Study
(1993–1994), 4, 6, 62; data analysis from, 44–62; data on long-
term support for black feminism
and, 140–155; determinates of
feminist support and, 78–79, 88;
measurement of black feminist
consciousness on, 45–46; and
measurement of political participation, 99–100, 105; selection of
respondents, 6
National Conference of Black Political
Scientists, 1
National Election Studies (University
of Michigan), 6
Nationalism, black, 4, 12, 131
The National Notes (newsletter), 95
National Woman's Suffrage Association, 42
National Women's Day, 120
Nation of Islam, 12
Networks: antislavery, 4; of comple-
mentary alliances, 128–129, 133;
issue advocacy, 94, 96, 132
Neubeck, Kenneth, 72
Nie, Norman, 22, 115

Olsen, Marvin, 96, 97
Olson, Lynne, 2
On Lynching (Wells-Barnett), 19
Oppression: effect of daily encounters
with on feminist perspectives, 70;
everyday experiences of, 11; gender, 8, 122, 137; interlocking systems of, 4, 8, 10, 14, 20, 22, 35,
39, 45, 49, 64, 66, 67, 73, 89, 94,
122, 134; lived experiences and,
14; race, 2, 8, 9, 84, 89, 122, 137;
resistance and, 39; sexual, 2; simultaneity of, 12, 14, 15, 22, 23,
29, 36, 39, 121, 123; strategies

against, 134; through lynching,
20; through rape, 20
Orfield, Gary, 71, 133, 137
Organizations: black female-led, 3;
charitable, 66; feminist, 29, 128,
129; policymaking, 29; post-civil
rights, 90; religious, 119; social,
116; women's, 120, 121

Painter, Nell, 43
Patriarchy: acceptance of, 57; benefits
for black men in, 71, 84; challenges to, 11; efforts to eliminate,
153; and male-female relationships, 10, 11, 56; men's movement to end, 13; struggle against,
12, 122; validated by black
church, 10, 11, 35, 56
Payne, Charles, 10
Pierce, John, 33
Political: activism, 11, 24, 65, 87, 89;
activities, 100; actors, 3; alliances, 66; attitudes, 35; behavior, 27–29, 35; campaigns, 33;
discontent, 102; effectiveness,
116; ideologies, 4; mobilization,
97; orientations, 35; participation, 27–29, 33, 34, 96–118;
philosophy, 3; preferences, 4; socialization, 134; trust, 28, 127
Political behavior, black, 165–166; age
and, 99; campaign activity, 106,
106tab, 108tab; communal activity, 106, 106tab, 108tab; contact
behavior, 105, 106, 106tab,
108tab; defining, 107, 108; determinates of, 149tab; education and,
99; future research in, 127–131;
gender differences, 99, 108,
108tab, 109, 111tab; gender
measurement in, 113tab, 114tab;
group consciousness and, 96–118,
127; income levels and, 97, 99;
individual resources and, 96; influence on public policy, 101; marital

status and, 98, 99, 104, 111; organizational involvement and, 95; race consciousness and, 96–118, 109, 110, 110*tab,* 111; religiosity and, 98, 99, 104; residential status and, 99, 105, 111; signing petitions, 100–101; socioeconomic status and, 96–118, 127; volunteerism and, 115; voting, 100–101, 105, 106, 106*tab,* 108*tab*; work experience and, 95

Political science: black perspective in, 1; black women's studies and, 1–17

Politics: black, 90; black women's participation in, 4; community-centered, 5; cooperative behavior among citizens in, 101; direct contact behavior in, 101; feminist, 68; gender differences in behavior of, 28; historical ideologies in, 4; initiative required, 100; lack of research in black feminist voices in, 1; presidential election turnout and, 100; resources necessary for participation, 100; signing petitions and, 100–101; voting and, 100, 101

Poverty, 9

Power: black, 64; relations, 91; unequal distribution of, 14, 49

Power discontent, 16, 22, 38; as determinate of feminist support, 71, 79, 83*tab,* 84, 87; race consciousness and, 97, 102

Prestage, Jewel, 26, 124, 128, 136

Race: "autobiography" of, 30; consciousness, 5, 23, 27–29, 97–98; discrimination, 9, 14; everyday experiences of, 11; identity, 12, 34, 36–39, 76–77, 85, 123; identity as determinate of feminist support, 83*tab,* 86*tab*; intersection with gender, 36–39; loyalty, 27;

naturalization of, 30; oppression, 8, 9, 84, 122, 137; prioritized over gender, 7, 44, 49, 56, 57, 58, 77; privilege, 74; social construction of, 29, 30; structural barriers and, 97–98; theorizing, 29–36

Racial: awareness, 33, 48; discrimination, 11, 32, 116; domination, 49; identity, 33; oppression, 2; pride, 66; profiling, 87; solidarity, 87; uplift, 27, 64, 94

Racism: in criminal justice system, 32; environmental, 90; group strategies in confronting, 98; unwillingness of early women's movement to oppose, 3

Ransby, Barbara, 10, 11, 91

Ransford, Edward, 95

Religiosity: black feminist consciousness and, 16; as determinate of feminist support, 77–78, 79, 83*tab,* 84, 86*tab*; gender equality and, 35; political participation and, 98, 99, 104, 149*tab,* 150*tab,* 151*tab*

Research. *See also* Analysis items and themes: black female intellectuals/political scientists and, 121, 141–155; in black feminist consciousness, 1; current limitations in, 127–131; demographic variables and, 80; on determinates of feminist support, 63–91; empirical, 12–13; future, 127–131; limitations of, 12–13; on long-term attitudes toward black feminism, 141–142; need for models containing all relevant variables, 127; omission of black feminist voices in, 5, 6; political, 1; on political participation, 97; practical implications of, 131–133; psychological involvement and, 128; significance of, 67–68, 136–137; socioeconomic variables and, 79

Residential status: as determinate of feminist support, 70–71, 79, 83, 83*tab*, 86*tab*; political participation and, 99, 105, 111, 149*tab*, 150*tab*, 151*tab*

Resistance: collective, 11, 89, 122; economic boycotts, 89; freedom rides, 89; individual, 89; necessary acts of, 11, 20; oppression and, 39; sit-ins, 89, 116; slave revolts and, 89; transformation of everyday experience into, 64

Richardson, Marilyn, 63, 64, 65

Roberts, Dorothy, 8, 71, 72, 73, 129, 132, 133

Robinson, Deborah, 11, 12, 13, 16, 27, 37, 38, 51, 77, 112

Robnett, Belinda, 10, 135

Romero, Lora, 65

Rosenstone, Steven, 97, 98, 99, 100, 101, 116

Roth, Benita, 129

Rothenberg, Paula, 9

Rowe, Audrey, 9

Sapiro, Virginia, 13

Schechter, Patricia, 20, 21

Schlozman, Kay, 109, 115, 116

Separate but equal doctrine, 19

Sex, interviewer: black feminist consciousness and, 16; as determinate of feminist support, 78, 79, 83*tab*, 85, 86*tab*, 87

Sexism, 49; in black church, 57; experienced by black/white women, 51; white/black comparability, 12

Sexual: discrimination, 116; harassment, 27; oppression, 2

Shange, Ntozake, 49

Shanley, Mary, 2

Shingles, Richard, 22, 23, 33, 97

Sidel, Ruth, 129, 132, 133

Simien, Evelyn, 4, 5, 112, 113, 114, 135, 140, 148, 154

Slavery, 2, 87, 93; and stereotypes of African American women, 72

Smith, Barbara, 10, 124

Smith, Jessie, 9

Smith, Robert, 90

Smooth, Wendy, 10, 27

Social: hierarchies, 9, 74, 89; justice, 11, 19; organizations, 116; protest, 65; reform, 132, 134

Socialization, sex role, 6, 26, 59, 130, 153

Socioeconomic status, 9; black political behavior and, 96–118; as determinate of feminist support, 71, 79; political participation and, 149*tab*, 150*tab*, 151*tab*; predisposition to psychological orientations supporting political activity, 96

Something Within: Religion in African-American Political Activism (Harris), 28, 35

Spelman, Elizabeth, 35

Springer, Kimberly, 29, 133

Stanton, Elizabeth Cady, 3, 21, 42, 43

Staples, Robert, 48

Stereotypes: affect on private/public spheres of life, 73; of African American women, 7, 8, 71, 72, 73; gender role, 35; negative, 73; in rating African American female faculty performance, 74–76

Sterling, Dorothy, 63, 65, 93, 94, 116

Stewart, James, 63, 87

Stewart, Maria, 13, 63–67, 87, 120, 121

Stone, Lucy, 21

Stone, Pauline, 9, 10, 11, 26, 56, 57, 70, 77, 124

Student Nonviolent Corrdinating Committee, 112

Suffrage: antiblack sentiment and, 42; hostility of women towards men on, 42; indefensible positions of

white female leadership in, 43;
"lesser" question of gender and,
41–44; universal male, 42, 43,
60; women's, 20, 21, 64, 95
Sundquist, Eric, 30
Surveys: lacking enough African
American opinion, 24–27

Tate, Katherine, 7, 12, 13, 16, 22, 23,
24, 27, 28, 32, 33, 34, 37, 38, 51,
52, 97, 115, 124
Taylor, Ula, 43
Terborg-Penn, Rosalyn, 2, 3, 60
Terrell, Mary Church, 13, 93–96,
116, 120, 121
Theory: black feminist, 3, 7–9,
19–40; of double consciousness,
29, 30
Third World Women's Alliance,
129
Thomas, Clarence, 11, 27, 67
Timpone, Richard, 98, 100
Togeby, Lise, 68
Tonry, Michael, 73
Truth, Sojourner, 13, 41, 43, 44, 65
Tucker, Tamelyn, 10
Turner, Caroline, 74
TuSmith, Bonnie, 74
Tyson, Mike, 11

Universalism, false, 36
University of Connecticut: Center for
Survey Research, 142
US Constitution: Fifteenth Amend-
ment, 41, 42, 43; Nineteenth
Amendment, 95

Vargas, Lucila, 74, 75
Verba, Sidney, 22, 96, 97, 98, 99,
100, 101, 105, 115, 116
Violence: domestic, 9, 137; vigilante
acts of, 20
A Voice from the South (Cooper), 1, 2
Voluntarism, 96; political participa-
tion and, 115

Walker, Alice, 21, 49
Wallace, Michelle, 49
Washington, Booker T., 20, 21, 120
Washington, Mary, 2
Waters, Kristin, 63, 64, 65
Weitz, Rose, 71, 72, 74
Welch, Susan, 109, 152
Welfare reform, 131, 132, 133.
See also Stereotypes
Wells-Barnett, Ida, 8, 13, 19, 20, 21,
65, 120, 121
White, Deborah, 72, 95
White, John, 20, 21
Wilcox, Clyde, 11, 13, 16, 23, 28, 68,
70, 71, 77, 103, 112
Williams, Linda, 11
Williams, Patricia, 8, 74
Williams, Sherley, 20
Wilson, William, 127, 133
Wing, Adrien, 10, 132
Wolfinger, Raymond, 96, 97, 98
Women, African American: analysis
of determinates of feminist support and, 82–87; blamed for so-
ciopolitical ills, 8; in charge of
private sphere, 35; class exploitation and, 84; commitment to
activism by, 123; comparitive
political orientations, 35; conflicts
of interest for, 27; cultural images
of, 8; decision-making authority
of, 26; differing experiences of
racism than black men, 22; differing experiences of sexism than
white women, 22; as "doers" and
"carriers," 35; "doubly bound,"
27, 28, 52; in education systems,
2; exclusion from clergy, 10, 35;
experience of sexism by, 71–76,
122; experiences shaping lives of,
66; forced to choose between race
and gender, 7, 27, 44, 49, 56, 60,
115, 153, 154; formation of clubs
and charitable organizations by,
66, 94; as heads of household,

Women, African American (*continued*): 26, 32, 124; integration of
political science perspectives of,
3; invisibility of, 4; labor participation of, 26, 124; lack of trust in
government by, 33; long-term attitudes toward black feminism,
140–155; marginalization of by
black male leadership, 3; measurement of self-worth by, 9;
participation in civil rights movement, 32, 33; as political actors,
3, 4; political behavior determinants, 27–29, 150*tab*; politicized
group consciousness of, 8; in
protest activities, 33; race oppression and, 84; race-sex correspondence in lives of, 2; racism within
women's movement and, 55*tab*,
58, 59, 60; sexism within black
movement, 55*tab*, 58, 59, 60;
shunned as representatives of civil
rights movement, 112; simultaneity of oppression and, 14, 15; in
social hierarchies, 9; specialized
knowledge of, 25; status deprivation of, 9, 121; stereotypes in faculty ratings, 74–76; stereotypes
of, 7, 8, 71, 72, 73; subordinated
to white women in occupational
structure, 56; support for
women's movement, 26; traditional housewife role and, 26, 76,
124; trust in government by, 127,
128; unrecognized political activities, 10; voter registration by, 33;
voting behavior of, 33, 128
Women, white: experience of sexism
by, 71, 122; marital status as
determinate of feminist support,
84; as norm against which
black women compared, 72,
73
Women's studies, black: in political
science, 1–17

Yee, Shirley, 43
Young, Iris, 35, 91

Zinn, Maxine, 35

Job #: 99209 -99208

Author Name: Simien

Title of Book: Black Feminist Voices

ISBN #: 0791467899 / 0791467902